Essential Teachings

His Holiness the Dalai Lama

Essential Teachings

His Holiness the Dalai Lama

Introduction by Andrew Harvey

Translated by Zélie Pollon
Edited by Marianne Dresser

North Atlantic Books
Berkeley, California

Essential Teachings by His Holiness the Dalai Lama

Copyright © 1995 by North Atlantic Books. Translated from Tibetan into French by Gonsar Tulku, Georges Dreyfus, and Anne Ansermet, published under the title *Enseignements essentiels* © Éditions Albin Michel S.A., Paris, 1976. A second French edition was published in 1987 under the title *L'enseignement du Dalaï-Lama*, and reprinted in 1989 under the original title.

North Atlantic Books
P.O. Box 12327
Berkeley, CA 94712

Cover photograph of His Holiness the Dalai Lama © 1994 by Don Farber
Cover and book design by Paula Morrison
Typeset by Catherine Campaigne
Printed in the United States of America by Malloy Lithographing

Essential Teachings is sponsored by the Society for the Study of Native Arts and Sciences, a nonprofit educational corporation whose goals are to develop an educational and crosscultural perspective linking various scientific, social, and artistic fields; to nurture a holistic view of the arts, sciences, humanities, and healing; and to publish and distribute literature on the relationship of mind, body, and nature.

Library of Congress Cataloging-in-Publication Data
Bstan-'dzin-rgya-mtsho, Dalai Lama XIV, 1935–
    [Enseignements essentiels, English]
    Essential teachings / His Holiness the Dalai Lama ;
    Introduction by Andrew Harvey ; translated by Zélie Pollon ; edited by
Marianne Dresser.
        p.   cm.
    ISBN 1-55643-192-9
    1. Enlightenment (Buddhism)—Requisites.   2. Rgyal-sras
Thogs-med Bzaln-po-dpal. 1295–1369. Rgyal-sras lag len so bdun ma.
3. Spiritual life—Buddhism.   4. Bodhisattvas.   5. Madhyamika
(Buddhism).   I. Pollon, Zélie.   II. Dresser, Marianne.
BQ4399.B774   1994
294.3'444—dc20
                                                    94-24038
                                                         CIP

Acknowledgements

We extend our heartfelt thanks to Andrew Harvey, Anastasia McGhee, and Steven Goodman for reading the translation at various stages and offering many helpful suggestions. We also wish to extend our gratitude to Jeffrey Hopkins for his excellent scholarly translation of "The Key of Madhyamika" published in *The Buddhism of Tibet* (Ithaca, NY: Snow Lion Publications, 1987). While the French version of this text, to which we closely adhered, differed significantly from Dr. Hopkins' version, his interpretation provided a helpful guide and check for our translation of this subtle and challenging text.

The Glossary was extensively revised from the original French version, with additional material and definitions adapted from *The Encyclopedia of Eastern Philosophy and Religion* (Boston: Shambhala Publications, 1986) and the Glossary in *The Words of My Perfect Teacher* by Patrul Rinpoche (San Francisco: Harper-Collins Publishers, 1994).

Contents

Introduction by Andrew Harvey ... ix

The Path of the Bodhisattva ... 1

First Practice ... 12

Second Practice ... 17

Third Practice ... 19

Fourth Practice ... 21

Fifth Practice ... 23

Sixth Practice ... 30

Seventh Practice ... 33

Eighth Practice ... 43

Ninth Practice ... 44

Tenth Practice ... 46

Eleventh Practice ... 52

Twelfth Practice ... 59

Thirteenth Practice ... 60

Fourteenth Practice ... 60

Fifteenth Practice ... 60

Sixteenth Practice ... 61

Seventeenth Practice ... 61

Eighteenth Practice ... 62

Nineteenth Practice ... 63

Twentieth Practice ... 64

Twenty-first Practice ... 65

Twenty-second Practice ... 66

Twenty-third Practice ... 70

Twenty-fourth Practice ... 72

Twenty-fifth Practice ... 72

Twenty-sixth Practice ... 73

Twenty-seventh Practice ... 73

Twenty-eighth Practice ... 74

Twenty-ninth Practice ... 74

Thirtieth Practice ... 75

Thirty-first Practice ... 75

Thirty-second Practice ... 76

Thirty-third Practice ... 77

Thirty-fourth Practice ... 77

Thirty-fifth Practice ... 78

Thirty-sixth Practice ... 79

Thirty-seventh Practice ... 79

The Key of Madhyamika ... 81

Glossary ... 121

Introduction

With a noble mind, pure and generous, we will spread joy around us, we will feel great peace and we will be able to communicate that to others.

THE FIRST WORDS of the Dalai Lama that I read, fourteen years ago, were: "Religion, in all its forms, has as its root endless compassion." I was in Ladakh, living in a small village in the mountains. A young Tibetan monk was visiting me and had brought me a picture and a book of the man he called Kündoun, "The Presence." The words—simple enough—sent a visceral shock through my body. That evening, my friend and I went to meditate in a ruined monastery above the village. There, on the wall of the grass-filled courtyard, was a representation, crude but vivid, of the Buddhist Wheel of Life. In the "hell" section, amidst flames and prowling savagely unhappy ghosts, stood a tall thin man surrounded by white light. "This is Avalokiteshvara," my friend said, "the Buddha of compassion. For Buddhists, hell is not final. It is as impermanent a state as all others. There is always a way out. *He* embodies that way." *Avalokiteshvara,* he told me, came from the Sanskrit *Avalokita,* "to preserve," and *Ishvara,* "Lord, or freedom," and so means "The Lord that protects." A warm summer moon rose and he spoke to me of the Mahayana Buddhist vision of the bodhisattva, the enlightened being who out of love returns again and again to the world to save all sentient beings. "The bodhisattva," he said, "has taken the most noble vow of all: not to enter nirvana until every creature—even the grass blades in this courtyard—have achieved enlightenment." We both laughed a little nervously as the grass blades looked particularly bedraggled and irredeemable. When we left, my Tibetan friend went up again to the Wheel of Life. "Here," he exclaimed waving to the ghosts wandering in garish flames, "is the modern world." He paused. "And here," pointing to the tall thin man now shining in the moonlight, "here is Kündoun." I could not help smiling at the extravagance of his devotion. He caught my smile and said, "You smile now but one day you will understand."

It has taken me fourteen years to begin to understand, and now that understanding is dawning in me I find it being shared by a startling variety of people from all over the world. One of the worst-kept modern secrets, it seems, is that the Dalai Lama is not merely the loved priest-king of the Tibetans, not just the world's most prominent Buddhist leader, but also a guide to the future that everyone, whatever their religion or lack of it, should take seriously. A Greek friend dying of AIDS in Paris told me, "I don't believe in anything but I believe in him," pointing to the one photograph by his bedside, that of the Dalai Lama. "I saw him once on television, and I felt that he was sane. I saw that there is no discrepancy between what he says, what he does, and what he is. I saw that although he had suffered everything a man can suffer—the death of those close to him, the destruction of his culture, the genocide of his people—he is not bitter. I do not believe in God but I believe in the power of love. He is that power." Later at his funeral, his lover turned to me and said, "Do you know what he told me when I asked him before the end how he could be so serene? He pointed to a picture of the Dalai Lama. 'He showed me

how,' he said. 'Don't ask me how. But he did.'" I remembered
the wall in Ladakh and the tall thin man moving calmly through
hell. I remembered him again in Venice a month later when a
German director at the première of his film announced, "There
is a world war going on between inner peace and outer nightmare, between force of mind and spirit and the force of power-
for-its-own-sake, between democracy and totalitarianism,
between life and death. The wisest fighter in this war—on
whose outcome everything depends—is the Dalai Lama." And
before an astonished audience he produced copies of his personal selection of the Dalai Lama's philosophy and distributed
them to everyone.

What, then, is the Dalai Lama's philosophy? It is Buddhism
purified to its simplest human essence, an essence that tran-
scends all barriers, all colors and creeds. It is a philosophy of
the most urgent, practical, active altruism constructed not in
a study but lived out at the center of a storm of violence. It is
in the deepest and widest possible sense a philosophy of peace.
The Dalai Lama has understood that there will be no future
worth living unless everyone now takes personal responsibility for their own inner lives and universal responsibility for the
pain and misery in the world. He has understood that none of
the major terrible problems that threaten survival of the earth
can be solved by merely institutional or political methods.
Humankind to survive has to undergo a massive and unprece-
dented change of heart, an ordered and passionate spiritual
revolution that changes forever our relation to each other and
our relation to nature. It is only from such a revolution that
the new vision the planet so desperately needs can arise—a
vision that sees the connections between every thought and
every action, the relations between the obsession with the individual self and its hunger for false securities and every kind of

exploitation that is ruining the world. As the Dalai Lama says so fiercely in *Essential Teachings,*

> Look around us at this world that we call "civilized" and that for more than 2,000 years has searched to obtain happiness and avoid suffering by false means: trickery, corruption, hate, abuse of power, and exploitation of others. We have searched only for individual and material happiness, opposing people against each other, one race against another, social systems against others. This has led to a time of fear, of suffering, murder, and famine. If in India, Africa, and other countries misery and famine rule, it is not because natural resources are lacking, nor that the means of bringing about lasting well-being are flawed. It is because each person has looked only for his own profit without fear of oppressing others for selfish goals, and this sad and pitiful world is the result. The root of this civilization is rotten, the world suffers, and if it continues in this way, it will suffer more and more.

The only way out of this hell, the Dalai Lama makes clear, is for each of us to take the journey of the bodhisattva into the heart of compassion, for every one of us to learn how to enact in whatever station of life we find ourselves that compassion and its forgiveness, clear insight, tolerance, humor, and tireless service to other beings. The only way out of this hell is to learn how to walk in it, as His Holiness does, with the calm passion of enlightened love.

The brilliant clarity and the interconnectedness of the Dalai Lama's analysis of the modern world would have less weight if he had not staked his whole life on its truth and if it had not been forged, as it has been, in the crucible of the forty-year- long nightmare of the destruction of the Tibetans by the Chinese.

His talk of forgiveness is the talk of one who has seen his people tortured and murdered in the hundreds of thousands; his belief in tolerance is the belief of one who has witnessed the annihilation of the whole religious world he came from by those who believe that "power comes from the barrel of a gun"; his amazing humorous clarity is of the kind reached only by those who survived hell, is as earned and weathered as Lear's, "a condition of complete simplicity," in Eliot's words, "costing not less than everything." When the Dalai Lama speaks he speaks not just for himself or for his tragic people, but for the humiliated and the noble of the earth, on behalf of the best in us all.

I first met the Dalai Lama in Oslo during the week in 1989 when he received—at long last—the Nobel Prize. I had been thinking about him for years but it was the first time I was continually in his presence—in processions, at speeches, at press conferences, at dinner. A kind of holy drunkenness—and in Oslo, of all places—reigned at every occasion. The Berlin Wall had just fallen and that the Dalai Lama should be receiving the Peace Prize soon afterwards seemed an almost hallucinatorily hopeful sign that the tide in world affairs might be changing. "Bliss it is in THIS dawn to be alive" an American friend wrote on my hotel door in red chalk and underneath, "Oslo, December 1989, is the Earthly Paradise." Every room the Dalai Lama walked into he touched, blessed, stroked, teased, enthused as many people as possible, radiating with every moment, every look, every word an unbreakable laughing compassion whose warmth pervaded everything. Tibetan representations of Avalokiteshvara show the bodhisattva with a thousand outstretched arms; the Dalai Lama seemed to have at least that many, and to be simultaneously present all over Oslo at once. No sooner had you glimpsed him at one end of the room, he would be at the other standing by you, looking deep into your eyes; no sooner had you just left him at a long press conference when he appeared round the corner in the rain, holding hands with two schoolgirls with red boots the color of his robe.

At moments he looked a hundred, a Tibetan Oedipus at Colonus; at others, seven or eight. He had the grace of a woman, the strength of a peasant, the contagious flagrant hilarity of a child, the eyes of a dolphin, sky-candid and serene. His laugh itself seemed superhuman, a burst of spontaneous coloratura that sliced through all pretension, all distance: some wag said, "When the Dalai Lama laughs, it sounds as if all the other thirteen Dalai Lamas are laughing with him." His face changed a hundred times an hour; yet there was always a stillness, a majesty in it that no change affected. I had seen hundreds of photographs of him but nothing prepared me for the beauty of this slender fifty-four-year-old man—not a cosmetic beauty at all but the kind that Ramana Maharshi or Gandhi had— the beauty of a totally good and loving being whose every ex- pression revealed another nuance of truth in action. Watching his face became a meditation as rich as listening to his words; its openness made it seem more intimate to me than that of my oldest friends.

The Dalai Lama's genius for joy inflamed the joy in every- one else; his smile reflected itself in a thousand faces at once. Words of an old Buddhist text kept coming back to me: "By giving away everything, pass beyond sorrow." Here was unmis- takably the most strongly and lucidly happy man I had ever seen giving himself and his wisdom away to anyone who could receive it. Hardly anyone seemed to sleep that crazy, glorious week. Bars and hotel rooms were full of people of all nationalities talking and joshing until the early hours. I met a distinguished economist on a street corner at three o'clock one morning weeping under his purple umbrella. "Why are you crying?" "I'm not sure. I think I'm going mad. I never even *imagined* one could be this *well*."

I met the Dalai Lama alone for forty-five minutes on the last day of my stay in Oslo. He sat at the end of a bare empty sunlit room in the early morning in a simple red and gold robe, his arms uncovered. He seemed unnervingly still, concentrated, immensely powerful—hardly a man at all, but a force of laser-like intensity. Then he looked up and laughed and my awe became laughter too. He put out his left arm and pulled me down gently onto the sofa beside him.

"What would you like the world to know about the Tibetan situation?" I began.

"That Tibet is not, has not ever been, and will never be legally a part of China. That the Chinese since 1950 have killed a quarter of the population—about 1.2 million people out of six million, as well as destroying almost all of the six thousand monasteries that once existed. I would like the world to know that if the Chinese continue with the population transfer program that they are implementing at the moment there will soon be many more Chinese in Tibet than Tibetans and then the destruction of Tibet will be complete."

He paused and added calmly, "There is not much time left."

There was a long sad silence. I told him that I considered the survival of Tibet as vital to the world's future as the survival of the rain forests of the Amazon. "The forests give the world oxygen; the Tibetans give the world an *inner* oxygen—of vision, of holy knowledge—that it needs to continue."

He smiled sadly. "The Tibetans have so much to offer to the world. An understanding of mental calmness, a vision of the infinite potential of the mind. You cannot talk of Tibet without talking of Tibetan Buddhism. This is essentially a collection of techniques for building inner peace through an expansion of consciousness. When has the world needed this more? If Tibet is not freed and the Tibetans not allowed to practice their culture and religion, this vision will die."

He gazed at his hands. "I want a free Tibet to be zone of *ahimsa*, of harmlessness, a sanctuary for peace where everyone can feel free to come and be refreshed. A place dedicated to the practice of compassion, of the way of the bodhisattva."

"What is compassion?" I asked him.

"To recognize yourself clearly in every other being and to respect each sentient being's right to happiness."

"Don't the Buddhists believe that the practice of compassion is the key to enlightenment?"

"Yes, because it breaks down all barriers of every kind and in the end destroys the notion of the separate self. But this is Buddhist business. Compassion is essential for everyone; it is the key to a happy life. A world without compassion is not a human world."

Then we talked about the dialogue between religion and science that he has advocated and the way in which Buddhism might be a bridge between the two.

"Some Westerners call Buddhism a science of mind," I said. "This is in some ways a helpful description. Buddhism is rational and the Buddha told everyone to test his truths for themselves. Both Buddhists and scientists are trying to *know* something essential about the universe and know it *clearly*."

"Buddhism may have a great role to play in being the necessary bridge between religion and science. In many ways Buddhism is like a religion although it does not believe in a creator god; in many ways, as I have said, it is like science. If science tells me that the world is round I accept it though some of the old texts say it is flat. If science can prove beyond any doubt that there is no reincarnation, for example, I will accept that too. One day soon perhaps more scientists will be open to what Buddhists may have to tell them of the powers of consciousness."

"And the survival of Tibet may be vital to this dialogue because the Tibetans have made the most sustained experiment in history into the nature of the mind."

"Yes."

I then asked him a question that had been haunting me all week. "You, as the most prominent Buddhist leader, talk always of tolerance, of listening to the truths of other religions. Yet the leaders of the other world religions—of Catholicism and Islam, for instance, and the Hindu fundamentalists—are very far from being tolerant. How can they change?"

He laughed. "Communism is very intolerant, isn't it? Communism *hates* capitalism. And yet all its hatred cannot destroy it. It is now having to find a way of coexisting with it. Some Christians and some Muslims, and certain Hindus, may sometimes be intolerant. Even if they are they cannot destroy other religions. The only practical and sensible thing is for all of us to sit down in friendship and discuss everything with respect. Reality is telling us quite clearly that we have to get together, to emphasize the unity of our common purpose and exchange our experiences. Exchange with another tradition can only lead to enrichment of your own. What is there to fear?"

"Have you learned anything from Christianity, for example?"

"Oh, so much," he said passionately. "Christianity has a very important and very beautiful sense of service. This service to other beings is essential. Buddhists too often think meditating is enough." He pulled a serious face and started to play with an imaginary rosary in his right hand. "Meditation is not enough. We must help others. Compassion must be active, otherwise it is lazy."

"Can you imagine a world religion ..."

His laugh cut me short. "No world religion. We have enough religions. Enough religions but not enough real human beings. We need more human beings. Religions should learn from each other, respect each other, but keep their identity. Some people like tomatoes; some people like bread. People should be free to eat what they want and people should be able to choose what religion is most useful to their growth. Don't let us talk too much of religion. Let us talk of what is human. Love is human. Kindness is human. Everyone needs love and kindness. A dog won't come near you if you're unkind to it. Our world is forgetting what is essential, what is essentially human." His voice rose richly on the word "human."

After a pause, I asked him if he knew violence within his own personality.

"Of course," he laughed. "*Now* I cannot watch a bird suffer without pain, but when I was a boy I killed several birds. In the Potala I kept some small beautiful birds in a cage. Hawks used to come and steal their food. According to my motivation, they had no right to eat those things. So I found a rifle which belonged to the Thirteenth Dalai Lama, transformed myself into a wrathful deity, and shot at one of them who fell to the ground in great pain. I felt great, great regret. Once violence is done, there is nothing that can be done to undo it. That afternoon I learned how sad that is."

"Is there a great soul-force in nonviolence, as Gandhi believed, a storing-up of karmic power that in the end can change fate?"

"Let us leave karma out of it," he smiled. "My belief is that nonviolence is simple realism. It is certainly realism in the Tibetan situation. The Chinese in the past have taken any slight outbreak of violence as an excuse to massacre thousands. But in any case whatever violence builds up, violence can destroy. Nothing that violence achieves is stable. This is a law. Only a wise, loving, patient intelligence can create anything that lasts; only altruism really helps. This is a law too. My definition of altruism is: be wisely selfish and know that your happiness depends on the happiness of those around you and the world in general. If society suffers you will suffer, so love yourself enough to work for the social good."

"You wrote once that you considered Gandhi's nonviolent way an 'introduction of an ancient practice of nonviolence into politics that represents an evolutionary leap for mankind.' Do you believe this still?"

"Yes. Look at what is happening in Eastern Europe. The Berlin Wall is down; so much has altered in Russia, also in a nonviolent way. Mrs. Aquino's change to democracy after the end of the Marcos regime was also largely nonviolent. Nonviolence is the only way for the oppressed people of the earth to move forward into a peace that could be lasting. When I first came to Europe in 1973 and talked like this people thought, 'Ah, well, the Dalai Lama, he is a little strange.' Now they are beginning to see that perhaps the Dalai Lama was not talking such nonsense after all."

He laughed a long time and then stood up. Our time was about to be over. I stood up and the Dalai Lama held my hand very strongly and tenderly in his left. Slowly, very slowly, in glowing silence, he walked me to the door. Then, with the deepest, most exquisite gentleness like that of a mother with a fragile, anxious child, he let slip my hand and said, very softly, "Goodbye."

As I walked away the face of my Tibetan friend returned with these three lines of a hymn to Avalokiteshvara he had written out for me, fourteen years before, on that evening in Ladakh:

> *Who flies unobstructed*
> *Through skies of limitless love?*
> *He whose mind is one with Reality . . .*

Back in Paris a few days later I was strolling through La Procure, the large religious bookstore in St. Sulpice, my mind and heart still full of the Dalai Lama, and I came across the French version of the book that is here translated into English. I bought it and read it over and over and gave copies away to all my friends. It became an indispensable book to me because in it I hear clearly the unsparing kind voice of the man I had met in Oslo.

Every time I gave a copy of the book away I used to say, "Here is the clearest guide I know to the mind of the most awake man on the planet." The first part is a series of talks given at Bodh Gaya to his own people on the sublime book of Shantideva, "On the Making of the Mind of the Bodhisattva." Because he is speaking to his own people, the Dalai Lama speaks directly, fiercely, unsentimentally, unedited by "political" considerations and with a pungent psychological brilliance and honesty that is always a part of his personality but more on display here than in any other published text of his I know. In a hundred or so magnificent and potent pages he introduces you to what it means to want with your whole being to attain enlightenment on behalf of all sentient beings and what it *costs* and *means*, in terms of aspiration, love, steady forgiveness of one's enemies, and relentless work on wearing down all those negative tendencies that separate all of us from each other.

In the second text, "The Key of Madhyamika," he discusses with precise intellectual brilliance—and in such a way that the committed reader can actually *glimpse* and feel through his presentation of the vision of emptiness something of its soaring freedom—how the greatest mystics of the Mahayana tradition have expressed their knowledge of the nature of reality. So in one small book you have marvelous representations of what the Tibetans call the two interpenetrating aspects of the enlightened mind: its boundless compassion and its "empty" wisdom.

I remember a moment in Oslo when His Holiness was speaking to a small group about the sufferings of Tibet and the modern world in general. For one unforgettable moment, his poise wavered and tears rolled down his cheeks and he said, "Compassion would be unbearable sometimes without the wisdom of emptiness." I often think of that moment and what he said when I think of the immense labor of transformation that faces the entire human race as it faces Apocalypse. On whether we learn how to unite compassion with the "wisdom of emptiness," how both to care enough and to work with enough selfless detachment in the middle of raging and devouring chaos, depends the future. To that future, this book is a wonderful gift, the gift of a wonderful man whose heart and mind are as spacious as the universe, and whose life is that of an authentic and humble hero of truth, who has put into practice day in and day out, in terrible and tragic conditions, the great prayer of the bodhisattva in Shantideva's *Bodhicharyavatara,*

*Like earth and the great elements and also vast as the
immensity of space,
Let me be the living ground of love for innumerable beings.*

Andrew Harvey
San Francisco, California
November, 1994

*I dedicate this introduction and all its meager merits, in love,
to Leila Hadley Luce, beloved friend and heart-champion
of the Tibetan cause.*

Part One

*The Path
of the Bodhisattva*

WHETHER WE ARE white, yellow, or black, whatever our social class and whatever our age, all of us—from human beings and animals down to the smallest insect—have the feeling that we are an "I." Even if we do not understand the nature of this "I," we nevertheless understand all that it desires: to avoid suffering and obtain happiness. We feel we have a right to happiness, and we do. The manifestations of suffering are innumerable and extremely varied, and we seek to protect ourselves from all of them. Animals also do this and in this way they very much resemble us. But they do not have foresight and lack the means to keep themselves from harm. So, while the basis of our motivation is the same—to avoid suffering and obtain happiness—we humans have many more ways of accomplishing it. The happiness we search for also takes many different forms, but fundamentally it is the same.

Our concept of "I" expands: we would like to obtain happiness for our family, "my" family, "my" friends, "my" country. Then what we call happiness and suffering takes on a much deeper and more vast meaning. Once our most immediate needs are satisfied, our notion of happiness changes slightly and the means of obtaining it become more complicated. The creation of language and literature, education and teaching, different social systems, the arts, schools and hospitals, factories, medical progress—everything comes from this one basic desire: to obtain happiness and avoid suffering. All life on earth participates in this quest.

Different philosophies try to answer and explain the questions posed by existence. In examining our nature and the order of the world, these philosophies hope to discover the real cause of happiness and suffering and find a solution. Certain philosophies are systematized in society and politics. Communism, for example, holds that attaining happiness and avoiding suffering can be accomplished by a system of equality among people in which the dominance of one social class, a minority exploiting the majority, will no longer exist. Religions try to resolve this eternal problem by explaining its cause according to their diverse points of view. We can distinguish doctrinaire views, those that look for an answer in causal and universal principals, from non-doctrinaire views which seek a practical solution in the social and material realms. In this sense, the Buddhadharma is doctrinaire.

We can observe that bodily suffering often comes from the mind, or that if two people are enduring an equal degree of physical suffering, one whose mind is calm and happy suffers much less than one whose mind is agitated and anxious. We can also see that even very fortunate people, who possess all that material well-being can bring, are depressed, anxious, and unhappy ... while others, whose daily lives are filled with misfortune yet who have a happy spirit and inner peace, give an impression of great serenity. A person whose mind is clear, open, and balanced will envision the frame of mind that she will adopt in the face of inevitable difficulties and will remain peaceful even if she experiences great pain, while a narrow-minded, agitated, and anxious person will unthinkingly become frustrated right away and lack resources when faced with the most minor unforeseen difficulty.

The mind is much more important than the body. So, since it is the state of our mind which to greater or lesser degrees allows us to endure or even just to experience suffering, this shows us that we should attach much greater importance to our way of thinking. The preparation of our mind is therefore extremely important and the practice of Dharma is excellent preparation. Let us put aside for a moment the law of karma and reincarnation and consider only the fruits that the practice of Dharma can bring us in this existence. Our own mind and especially the minds of others will reap the fruit. With a noble mind, pure and generous, we will spread joy around us, we will feel great peace and we will be able to communicate that to others.

Look around us at this world that we call "civilized" and that for more than 2,000 years has searched to obtain happiness and avoid suffering by false means: trickery, corruption, hate, abuse of power, and exploitation of others. We have searched only for individual and material happiness, opposing people against each other, one race against another, social systems against others. This has led to a time of fear, of suffering, murder, and famine. If in India, Africa, and other countries misery and famine rule, it is not because natural resources are lacking, nor that the means of bringing about lasting well-being are flawed. It is because each person has looked only for his own profit without fear of oppressing others for selfish goals, and this sad and pitiful world is the result. The root of this civilization is rotten, the world suffers, and if it continues in this way, it will suffer more and more.

Some people who have a lot of weighty cultural and intellectual baggage and consider themselves open-minded think that the Dharma is without use or that it is good only for those living in undeveloped and isolated areas. But what is the Dharma?

Obviously it is not wearing special clothes, building monasteries, and devoting oneself to complicated rituals. These things
can accompany the practice of Dharma, but are not, in any
way, *the* Dharma. The true practice of the Dharma is internal;
it is a peaceful, open, and generous mind, a mind that we know
how to train, that is completely in our control.

Even if we can recite the entire *Tripitaka* by heart but are
egotistical and do harm to others, we are not practicing the
Dharma.

The practice of Dharma is that which allows us to be real,
faithful, honest, and humble — to help and respect others and
sacrifice ourselves for them. Trying to accumulate possessions
or achieve a better social status will not bring you faith or peace.
Some people bend very low before the powerful of this world,
flattering them as much as possible while criticizing and despis-
ing them behind their backs. Those who stir up craving often
do not have a calm mind and are anxious and distraught at the
thought of losing what they have been able to acquire at great
cost. When we die we will have to leave everything behind us,
even the most solid material foundation that has given us so
much trouble to achieve. We will also have to leave our parents
and friends. If our life has been dishonest we may feel great
regret, but in any case we cannot profit from the fruits of our
dishonesty. We must leave our bodies. My body also, that of
Tenzin Gyatso, I must leave it and my monks' robe which I
have not been without for even a single night. So we will leave
everything, and if our only possessions were material and selfish, our last moments will be troubled by anxiety and sorrow.

Training our mind, renouncing excess, and living in har-
mony with others and with ourselves will assure us happiness,
even if our daily life is ordinary. And if we should encounter
adversity, others will help us because we will have been good

and kind. We must not forget that even in the most perverted and cruel human being, as long as he is human, a small grain of love and compassion exists that will make him, one day, a Buddha.

Now we must also think of our next life. The law of karma is not easy to understand, nor is reincarnation. But if we very carefully examine the facts of existence, with an honest mind and without taking sides, we will understand them. And we will also refer back to the teachings of the Buddha which affirmed reincarnation.

Everything that happens, individually or collectively, happens because of the law of karma. The good path we have followed will bear fruit in the next life, the effort that we made will allow us to obtain a noble and pure mind. Your having come here proves my words, because you have come to receive teaching concerning the Dharma, which shows that for you the Dharma has meaning. Dharma is equivalent to goodness; if someone rejects the Dharma, it is because he does not understand this. The Dharma is the only possibility of obtaining happiness.

Each religion has a Dharma; of these, the Buddhadharma was taught by the Buddha. A thousand Buddhas will appear in this *kalpa;* Gautama Buddha is the fourth. He lived in the country where we now find ourselves, and it was in this exact place that he attained enlightenment. After enlightenment, he turned the "Wheel of the Law" for the first time at Sarnath, and then turned it several more times before entering *parinirvana.* He taught both ordinary people whose understanding was limited as well as disciples whose minds were more open. He taught to public gatherings and to secret assemblies. He taught other worlds. He taught the *devas.* His teachings were staged at different levels and their meanings ranged from being very accessible to everyone to those that were very profound and difficult to understand.

The teachings included both Hinayana and Mahayana; the Mahayana is greater in its motivation, its practices, and its objective. Its motivation is that of happiness for all sentient beings instead of just one's own well-being. The practice of six or ten *paramitas* accompanies the Mahayana. And the goal of this teaching includes not only liberation from samsara but also attainment of the three *kayas: nirmanakaya, sambhogakaya,* and *dharmakaya.* The Mahayana Dharma includes the paths of Paramitayana and Vajrayana. The latter has different qualities that make it superior to the sole practice of the paramitas, but the union of both is very important.

We are fortunate because Buddhism came directly to Tibet from India, so we have an authentic and complete Dharma. According to a prophecy of the Buddha, the Dharma must go from South to North: Tibet, Mongolia, China, and Japan; it seems that the trajectory is finished, I don't know if there is yet another North! Throughout its history, the Buddhadharma has prospered during some periods, and almost disappeared at other times.

During Gautama Buddha's lifetime, the Hinayana flourished because it was easy to comprehend and so could be taught to numerous listeners. The Mahayana, which demanded a better-prepared mind, was less popular and was taught only to more advanced disciples. This is why it was criticized, and its existence in early Buddhism was contested and still is by some. However, the Mahayana really existed from the very beginning in Gautama Buddha's first turning of the Wheel of Dharma. After the parinirvana, it seemed to have disappeared for several centuries. The Mahayana had a resurgence at the time of Nagarjuna.

Nagarjuna was the restorer of the Mahayana. His coming had been prophesied by the Buddha in several sutras, particularly the *Manjushri Mulatantra*. Nagarjuna lived about 400 years after the Buddha. From that time, the Mahayana has known a great expansion, then renewal, several centuries after it had degenerated. Eventually, Buddhism disappeared almost completely from India. Since its arrival in Tibet and until recently, Buddhism has always existed in our country. It was overshadowed for nearly eighty years during the reign of Langdar-ma, but even during this time it survived in the eastern and western parts of the country. Later it also had periods of recession, but we can say that for a thousand years the pure tradition of Dharma, which is the union of the Paramitayana and the Tantrayana, has continued in Tibet.

We have different schools, in some cases named for the time at which they were formed, after a specific place, or after their founder or teachings.* All of these schools follow the same tradition, the union of the paramitas and the tantras. There are minor differences in the interpretation of this method and in the application of certain practices, but the essence is the same. The practice, the method of the Tibetan Mahayana, and its teaching unifies the sutras and tantras aimed at cultivating *bodhichitta*. The aspiration of bodhichitta is the foundation of the Paramitayana and its ultimate goal is the realization of *shunyata*. In order to practice the Tantrayana, it is absolutely necessary that we have the aspiration of bodhichitta.

Bodhichitta is the necessary motivation for a successful transformation of the mind. The path begins with the renunciation

---

*For example, the Nyingma-pa school is named "for the time at which it was formed"; Sakya-pa and Kagyu-pa are schools named "after a specific place."

of the samsaric state, continues through the development of a spirit of love and compassion, the stage called "relative bodhichitta"; and then comes the realization of the ultimate nature of reality: shunyata, or at least a conceptual understanding of it. It is not until this point that we may approach tantrism, which consists of two stages: generation, then accomplishment, which provides us with the genuine fruit. The fruit cannot ripen except through this process. Without the three bases (renunciation, bodhichitta, shunyata), the meditations on the deities (entities of the path) and the exercises on the *nadis* will not only be useless but can be harmful, even if, technically, we know how to practice them.

The preparation for our development by tantrism is therefore very important. It is not only necessary to understand the significance of renunciation, bodhichitta, and the realization of emptiness, but to meditate on them at length, to become "pregnant" with them and integrate them into our minds. Only after this can the tantric path be profitable. The most essential of these preliminary realizations is bodhichitta, which is why I offer you today the teaching of Guru Thogs-med bsang-po.

Thogs-med bsang-po was a very great lama, humble and patient, overflowing with love and compassion for all beings. He was accompanied by a wolf that followed him like a faithful dog and whose nature he had transformed—the wolf actually became vegetarian! And when this master gave teachings on bodhichitta, the suffering of beings was so present in his mind that tears flowed from his eyes. He studied at the Sakya Monastery and renounced the world late in life, withdrawing into solitude in order to develop bodhichitta more completely.

His teaching was given to me by Lama Koundo (Tenzin Gyaltsen) who received it himself from the abbot of the Dzogchen Monastery.

The introduction to the "Thirty-seven Practices of the Sons and Daughters of the Buddha" is an homage addressed to Avalokiteshvara under the name of Lokeshvara. He is the object of this homage because the verses describing the practices of the bodhisattva are based on great compassion, and Avalokiteshvara is the source of this great compassion.

Remember that the three doors of the Buddha are Manjushri (wisdom), Vajrapani (ability), and Avalokiteshvara, who represents the collective compassion of all Buddhas.

This homage is also addressed to the guru because, as Atisha has said, all qualities, great and small, are due to the guru. In particular, the Mahayana qualities come from the guru; it is only through him or her that we are able to find the appropriate method for our own development and that is why we take refuge in the guru.

Here is the text:

> *Homage to Lokeshvara.*
>
> *Before those who have seen that all phenomena are without going or coming and who dedicate their efforts for the benefit of all beings; before the supreme gurus; and before you, Lokeshvara the Protector, I respectfully bow down, paying homage through my three doors (body, speech, and mind).*
>
> *The Victorious Buddhas, from whom all happiness and goodwill come, have attained their realization by the practice of Dharma, which itself depends on our understanding of it. I will therefore explain the practices of the bodhisattva.*

The guru and Avalokiteshvara addressed in this homage are not ordinary beings. They form an "object of refuge" which concentrates all kinds of realization.

Renunciation is not just for those who have passions and delusions, but also for those for whose minds still contain even the slightest trace of illusion. Even the great arhats are unable to see the two truths—the relative and the absolute—simultaneously. Meditatively absorbed in emptiness, they are unable to see phenomena clearly; or they may perceive phenomena but do not "see" emptiness even if by chance they have realized it in meditation. Only one who has arrived at buddhahood can see both at the same time. In order to do this, he or she will have completely abandoned all traces of illusion. He or she knows that there is no going or coming; that ultimate shunyata is constant.

Avalokiteshvara's qualities permit him to help all sentient beings, according to their own capacities and their own state of awakening, to practice this meditation on the union of the realization of emptiness and the perception of all phenomena. This is why not only today but always, completely, through my three doors, I take refuge in Avalokiteshvara and pay homage to him.

First Practice

The possession of this human base, this precious vessel so difficult to obtain, in order to liberate others and ourselves from the ocean of samsara, allows us to hear, reflect, and meditate day and night without distraction. This is a practice of the bodhisattva.

True happiness comes only through virtuous karma, the accumulation of virtuous acts producing "seeds" in the mind that grow into good possibilities. The way to eliminate errors is to give birth to the buddhamind within us—bodhichitta. To attain buddhahood we must learn to practice the Dharma, to know what must be abandoned and what must be practiced, and a precious human body is necessary for this. As I have been giving this teaching, there are many animals around us; theoretically, they should be able to hear it, but their animal state prevents this and they cannot understand anything. We are lucky to have obtained the necessary foundation of a human life. We have obtained it in a country where Dharma flourishes; we have the potential to read, to listen, to think, even to discriminate.

So we have all the faculties needed to practice the Dharma. Even if among you there is a very old person who does not know how to read or write, he can all the same listen to and understand some of these words concerning the Dharma. An old and worn-out body is still a precious human body, more precious than the most beautiful body of a young and healthy animal. Human life is of great value because there are many millions of lives on this earth, so the opportunity of obtaining a human body is rare. Those of us possessing a human body in this time, other Tibetans, and other people we encounter can know the complete Dharma, tantric Mahayana. Do not let this opportunity pass; to do so would be as absurd as if a starving person were to go with some money into a well-stocked market and return empty-handed. Whether we are young or old, every one of us must make the necessary effort and not waste this precious human life.

This human life, so difficult to obtain and so easy to lose, requires certain conditions. Some of these conditions arise from virtuous actions done in a previous life, not isolated and superficial good deeds, but frequent and repeated virtuous actions. We must begin now—not tomorrow or later—to build up merit. Our merit is quickly destroyed by the most minor fault of pride, animosity, egotism—feelings that we all have and that invade us promptly at any moment. It is therefore very doubtful that past merit, through which we have obtained this life, remains intact. Let us renew and increase our merit without thinking of the "capital" we believe we have acquired.

It is possible for each of us to practice the Dharma, because it does not involve an obligation to give up everything and go meditate in a cave. We can practice the Dharma in our daily lives by making some of our actions in the world spiritual ones. We must have a noble mind, one that is benevolent, open, not agitated or combative, and which will allow us to advance more quickly on the path when external circumstances are favorable. Begin this evening, do not wait until later. Awaken to the small faults that seem inoffensive at first; for example, become aware of the smallest lies—people lie at every opportunity, without thinking of the harm and without even realizing themselves that they are lying. These are karmic tendencies; we must undo them little by little and not become discouraged. Do not say, "The Dharma is too great for me, I am a sinner." We are all poor sinners and beginning this very evening we are nevertheless going to try to change a little. Starting now, I am also going to look at the faults that remain in me. Do this also and don't let things go on as before with the excuse that you are incapable.

To practice the Dharma is to gradually eliminate errors and increase true qualities in order to finally acquire the supreme qualities. At that moment, our capacity to help all sentient beings will be complete. Buddhahood comes from the practice of Dharma and this state is the only one that enables us to achieve ultimate and true happiness. We have the example of the bodhisattvas and Buddhas to help us understand this perfect fruit of the practice of Dharma. But we follow this path not just to gain intellectual knowledge of the Dharma; the necessary qualities develop only through practice and so it is very important to know what should be put into practice.

To arrive at a perfect practice allows us to help sentient beings according to their capacities. Avalokiteshvara possesses this perfection, which is why, according to the text, "I take refuge in him, not only today, but always and not only by my words but through the three doors of my being . . . I pay homage to him and I bow before him. . . ."

All happiness and peace come from "white" karma, a noble karma produced by the accumulation of right actions. So, again, the only path to follow, the only method, consists of eliminating wrongful acts, speech, and thought. Tsong Khapa said: "Even if my body perishes and my life ends and even if I must lose them because of the practice of Dharma, may I, despite everything, practice Dharma."

The Dalai Lama addresses the laypeople: When not receiving teachings, you should try to spend your days virtuously here at Bodh Gaya. We usually practice circumambulating the stupas; during these walks think of awakening the aspiration of bodhichitta in your mind. The *Bodhicharyavatara* says, "Like earth and the great elements and also vast as the immensity of space, let me be the living ground of love for innumerable beings." This prayer will make your circumambulation of the stupas very beneficial. Remember the Buddha, visualize him, think of his teachings, think of his compassionate love, and make a vow to follow the same path. In this way the strength of your motivation will be increased.

Then, addressing the monks: Living in a monastery, wearing a monk's robe, occupying yourselves with advanced practices, *pujas,* tantric rites—all this seems at first to be practicing the Dharma. But if the mind is distracted by minor external things of the world, all this amounts to nothing. Sometimes during important pujas I notice people around me who are distracted, obviously absorbed in mundane worries, but who outwardly appear virtuous. I think, "What a pitiful state they are in!" and I feel discouraged. Practicing the Dharma does not depend on our external appearance but on our state of mind and our inner motivation. The mind must be free of all frivolous thoughts, pure and completely engaged in whatever practice it is doing, so that even one hour of practice becomes very valuable.

Therefore even an old person, sick and weak, should not be discouraged and should try according to his or her own capability. Every opportunity is offered us — and why? Because we have received this precious human life.

Addressing everyone: Therefore, as soon as we have this opportunity, this good fortune — an adequate body and the necessary means — we must fully utilize these excellent circumstances by making great efforts to attain nirvana and buddhahood for the good of all sentient beings. The efforts we make for the good of all beings should flow like a river. The correct method is to first study in order to gain the necessary knowledge, then meditate on the Mahayana teachings, reflect on them, analyze what we have learned, investigate until we have obtained complete faith, and then concentrate our minds on that clear faith. We should alternate analytical meditation and calm, one-pointed concentration of the mind, in equal practice. Meditating in this manner, that we will gain an intuitive understanding.

So first, we must study. But this is not enough; we must contemplate and analyze and finally meditate deeply. In this way we will get good results. Do not separate these three exercises, but practice them in alternation.

The study of Dharma is not in the least like a kind of science, for example, history. Practicing the Dharma requires applying the methods of the Dharma, and this is the practice of the bodhisattva.

Second Practice

Toward our friends and those we love run the waters of attachment, toward our enemies burns the fire of aversion; in the obscurity of ignorance, we lose sight of what should be abandoned and what should be practiced. Therefore, renunciation of one's country and home is a practice of the bodhisattva.

In order to be capable of accomplishing the preceding practices, it is useful and sometimes absolutely necessary to leave our home and country. This helps cut the natural attachment we have for those around us, our family and friends. This gives us distance from the turmoil, the worries and daily nuisances connected to living in a social environment of objects, conditions, and circumstances which give rise to illusions. Living at home we are required to spend a lot of time working, for good or bad. A *tulku* has his family, his disciples, and many people who ask for his help. Even if he wants to remain tranquil he cannot, called upon by so many people and circumstances and also by the emotions they bring to him. All the possible reactions he might have to either praise or disdain, these are all temptations that come from those around him, even if they are perfectly blameless.

All the same, we must be mindful of the obscurity of ignorance, which does not allow the "leisure" of knowing what must be abandoned and what must be accepted. There are some monks who live very simply in tiny, poor rooms that are not much bigger than a mousehole, yet who have the same problems, worries, and useless anxieties as if they lived in luxury in a big city. They scurry about like ants, collecting old rags and bottles that they lovingly care for, amassing useless objects, and spending all their time searching for small treasures. This isn't bad in itself, but actually does no good whatever. They clean the cobwebs very carefully from the sacred books on their small altars, but they don't read them—preferring instead to polish the altar bowls! Their minds become attached to these objects and are distracted from practice.

Just as even the least irritation is a basis for aversion, so too even the smallest, seemingly natural desire can turn into incessant and ever-increasing greed. Any basis of attachment, however small, must be abandoned. If we could occupy ourselves externally with worldly things while our mind remains able to practice the Dharma internally without interruption, this would be very good. But this is difficult and generally not the case; consequently "to leave one's home is a practice of a bodhisattva." The home is where attachment is strongest and temptations the most powerful, because they are the most appealing to us.

The three poisons are desire, aversion, and ignorance. Ignorance comes first and has two accomplices: desire and aversion. Ignorance is a king who uses aversion to repel its enemies and desire and attachment to increase its power. If we meet someone and instantly feel repelled by them, aversion immediately arises. Our aversion makes us want to protect ourselves from them and assert ourselves against them, while actually this only brings failure. Attachment is an ally of gracious manners, sweet and pleasant, but its real nature is to deceive us. So be aware that ignorance, aversion, and attachment are called the three poisons for good reason, and when we notice that one of their deepest roots is house, home, and country, leaving these is a practice of the bodhisattva.

Third Practice

When we abandon our harmful surroundings, our illusions diminish, and because we have no distractions our practice of virtue develops spontaneously, leaving us with a clear mind. Our trust in the Dharma grows. To live in solitude is a practice of the bodhisattva.

However, to leave one's homeland only to find similar conditions in a faraway place or another country—to find a similar environment and new distractions—is obviously not the goal. (We Tibetans can attest to this: we have lost our country and our homes yet for so long have not lived in solitude but are surrounded by friends, family, and the same risk of external temptations.) We leave home with the goal of obtaining peace of mind, and obviously we are not going to find this in a noisy and frenetic city. We must search for a solitude blessed with the qualities described in the *Bodhicharyavatara*, which we found easily in Tibet—a pure and wholesome climate, silence, clean water, beautiful, serene nature inhabited by gentle animals, peaceful as deer. There, nothing can distract us; we can practice and reflect from morning until evening and contemplation will become a good habit. This solitude is very necessary; all the gurus of the past arrived at their high spiritual states only by leaving everything to practice the Dharma. And even if we are unable to complete this project now, we must keep it present in our minds. We must have this motivation: "One day, I will leave everything, I will go into solitude brandishing the banner of meditation."

Turning toward the monks: The monks should pay constant attention. Living in the monastery, we are the object of devotion and offerings and we participate in many pujas. These rituals, while they are very useful, can become dangerous for a mind that lets itself become distracted or absorbed by the desire for offerings that accompany them. If we eat too much and lead too sedentary a life, we do not purify ourselves and monastic life becomes dangerous, as well. Comfort, lack of responsibility, and rich food make the mind heavy, clouded, and dull. These temptations can be avoided by living in solitude. Eating moderately leaves the mind clear, and silence is favorable for realization.

Being an object of devotion is dangerous; it is also dangerous to anticipate offerings or gifts and to then instinctively show greater consideration and respect to those who give us more than others (who may have more sincere devotion, but less means). When we are ordained as a monk, our work is to follow the example of the Buddha, the great arhats, and gurus—to fight illusions and to renounce all worldly things and all samsaric pleasures. It is only at this moment that we become a true monk— it is not the act of putting on a robe that makes one a monk.

The objects of this world are the messengers of Mara, and as a Kadampa *geshe* said, a monk should be free and unfettered, like a bird. A monk should have a simple daily life; he should have just enough to live and eat, without excess. Only the special circumstances in which we live, in a world without Dharma, require that we sometimes appear otherwise. Monks have to teach others and their lives should be in accordance with their teachings. If we have the same illusions and attachments as those who listen to us, our words will not only be useless but harmful. If we live purely and free of attachments in a monastery, the sangha becomes a "field of merit" and the Dharma is well represented. The existence of Dharma depends on the quality of the community that practices it. Based on our philosophy, you should abide in the Middle Way without ever falling into extremes.

Monks and laypeople should help one another. In these times, monks must not only teach religion but all essential knowledge, and laypeople should help them, which is perfectly normal.

If we cannot at this time live "in solitude" we must at least live in a manner that allows us to remain peaceful and serene even in difficult surroundings.

Fourth Practice

One day old and dear friends will separate, goods and riches obtained by great effort will be left behind. Consciousness, a guest of the body, this temporary dwelling, will depart. From this moment on, to renounce all attachment to this life is a practice of the bodhisattva.

Let us say we have searched for solitude and found it, and that we have abandoned our home. This is not all we have to abandon. We must renounce our attachment to this temporal life, we must see that this existence is impermanent, whether it ends soon or later. Death will separate us from everything. To prepare for this departure, nothing else can be of use except the practice of Dharma.

If we have acquired a noble mind, this will help us. Even our closest friends cannot help; we may have all the friends in the world and they could do nothing for us. Even if we are as rich or as high a class as Vaishravana, still nothing will remain for us when we die.

This body, which is always with us and is precious to us, must be left behind. We do not know when this will happen. Human life is uncertain; young people naively say, "I am young and healthy, so I will go on living." This is neither reason nor proof. Out of all of you here, regardless of your age, not one person can affirm with 100 percent certainty: "I will be alive tonight." In short—we will all die, we have no idea when, and, aside from the practice of Dharma, there is no escape from this fact. So detaching yourself from the bonds of this life is valuable and useful, while the contrary is harmful. If we were to die this evening, we could prepare ourselves for this passage; and if we were to continue living, all the better. In any case, our preparation will not have been in vain.

This life, in itself, is not very important, but we constantly worry about it. The troubles in Tibet brought us here, we had to leave everything, and many people did not know from day to day what they would have to do. Nevertheless, we are still here in this human realm, and each of us has the opportunity to be here. So our worries were exaggerated. What is far more important is the moment when, separated from this world, we will travel alone into an unknown realm.

The Seventh Dalai Lama said in a prayer, "Beyond this world, we will be at an immeasurable distance from the things and people we are familiar with. In this human life, regardless of what happens, we can find help. In the *bardo,* we will be completely alone. We must know this and be prepared for it."

The Buddha said, "I show you the path to liberation, but it is up to you to take it."

Many people come to me and ask, "Pray that I do not fall into the hell realm." Of course I pray, with all my heart—even if I do not visualize each person individually, I pray earnestly for all. May I help them, help all of you a little. But according to the Dharma, each person is responsible for himself. I cannot pull someone from the hell realm and carry them to nirvana. Leaving samsara, attaining nirvana or buddhahood, depends on your own efforts. You cannot rely on anyone—not the guru, or the Buddha and bodhisattvas. They all would like to help all beings completely, but this is difficult and your cooperation is absolutely necessary. In acknowledging impermanence, in seeing the inexorable future that will become the present, you will prepare yourselves and come to understand that engagement in the ways of the world is a waste of your life. With this energy, this willingness, this constant and firm desire to practice the Dharma and not waste time, your attachment to this world will diminish and will in the end completely fade away. You will feel no anguish when faced with the passage of time.

"Not parents, or friends, or the greatest earthly love—at the moment of death, we will no longer possess anything, not even a name."

This body is a temporary dwelling, we cannot stay in it permanently. Our consciousness is present like a guest in the body. But this guest-consciousness, this eternal voyager, will depart one day; it will leave behind the shelter it received.

Friends, our body, even our name—nothing that we are attached to will exist. Therefore, abandoning all attachment is a practice of the bodhisattva.

Fifth Practice

If we have harmful companions, the three poisons are increased, our reflection and meditation becomes degraded; love and compassion are destroyed. To abandon dangerous company is a practice of the bodhisattva.

If we follow a false guru, the qualities developed previously grow weaker while our illusions become more compelling. We can recognize a false guru or a false spiritual friend by these signs: our ignorance will become more dense and our three practices *(shila, samadhi, prajna)* will weaken.

On the Mahayana path, in particular, we must pay attention and not let ourselves be influenced by friends and companions who have neither love nor compassion or who have lost them, for the essence of the Mahayana is love and compassion. To abandon these harmful friends is a practice of the bodhisattva.

In order to be able to attain buddhahood, nothing is more important than following the guru; this was emphasized by the great Guru Potowa. We must ask for teachings and help. This is important even if we are already "on the path," and especially important if we have just emerged from the hell realm. To follow the guru, through whom we see our faults and through whom our qualities will increase like "the crescent moon," to hold the supreme guardian as more worthy than one's own life, is a practice of the bodhisattva. For in order to develop our still-obscured mind, we must adopt a method and know how to follow it. The guide must be a perfect guru who shows us the path and teaches the method. He or she must have great experience so that we will have complete confidence in them. A person who is ill tries to find the best doctor and follows the prescribed treatment. The illness of the three poisons is far more dangerous than any disease of the body.

A trustworthy guru must possess certain qualities. The Sakya Pandita said, "We ask for advice and take elaborate precautions just to buy a horse.... All the more reason for us to be careful when it comes to our own eternal being." Before accepting a guru, before deciding if he or she will be the one or not, we must know the inherent qualities of a guru according to the *Vinaya,* the sutras, and the tantras, and we should only follow someone who has most of these qualities.

When we have found the true guru, we must follow them as if they were the equal of the Buddha, placing the guru in even higher regard, because of their kindness. With this clear vision we must develop a great and strong devotion from the bottom of our heart: devotion by perceiving the guru's qualities, respect by perceiving his or her goodness, adoration by observing both.

We should manifest this adoration by practicing exactly what the guru shows us. We can please the guru in three ways: by making offerings, by the services we render to him or her, and by our practice. But if the guru is a true guru, as they should be, they will be made much happier by a disciple's practice than by their offerings.

Marpa had two disciples: one who was very rich and gave Marpa all that he owned, and Milarepa, who had nothing at all. Marpa made no distinction between the two, saying: "My disciple Milarepa has nothing and my other disciple has given me everything, down to the last lame goat of his flock, but I make no distinction between them in the teachings I give them."

Sharawa said that disciples should give offerings in adoration to the guru, but the guru should not concern himself with the offerings, otherwise he could not be considered a Mahayana guru. To follow a guru correctly is a practice of the bodhisattva.

The first day of teachings is completed. We are now on the second day of teachings, which begins with an introduction followed by a summary of what has been previously said.

Second Day of Teachings

"The three worlds are as impermanent as autumn clouds; birth and death are like a game, like the swift waves of a cascading mountain waterfall." All conditioned phenomena, all beings, all places, are impermanent and changing. Not a single thing is eternal. Human life is a rudimentary and crude form of impermanence; it is terribly uncertain, particularly in this age. From the moment we are born we can be certain that we will die, and from that instant we approach death with each second. Death will arrive like a brutal bolt of lightning without our foreseeing or expecting it. Since the beginning of this world, people have been born, then die. Sometimes they have been wise, sometimes powerful; not one avoided the conditions of nature. Birth and death are those conditions.

Each being passes through the same process of degeneration. When we are very young we have no need of eyeglasses — I didn't used to have them and yet today I wear them, and my sight will fail more and more until I will not be able to see anything at all! The body is always degenerating, wrinkles appear, hair falls out, hearing becomes less acute; the more the body shrivels, the more we feel tired — tired of everything. Young people will take our place, regarding our ideas as old-fashioned and proudly imposing theirs over those of the Buddha. However, those who now treat us as driveling old fools will follow the same path. All the things we tasted with delight when young become disgusting to us; objects of attachment can also become objects of aversion. We are full of regrets because we had so many worthy plans that we were never able to fulfill. We no longer have the strength or the courage to complete the plans we made with such enthusiasm and energy, when we thought we could "catch the birds flying in the sky."

This time passes quickly. If we are laypeople, we get married and our spouse and children bring additional responsibilities. We expend our energy trying to achieve a better social standing, a better professional rank. Obtaining these things does not happen without a feeling of separateness arising — competition, jealousy, and then real malice when we have finally succeeded in making our "place in the sun." We cannot have done this without having pushed others to the side! In occupying yourself with these things, days pass, then years. . . .

The same can be true even for a monk in Tibet. There were certainly many students who worked with the motivation of attaining buddhahood, who were looked after by good gurus and had good companions. But some of the younger monks worked only toward temporal goals: to become a well-read scholar, a distinguished pandit, to gain the highest rank of geshe. With only this as the motivation, the rank of geshe is, as we say in Tibet, an "empty" title. A certain number of students nevertheless desired this "empty" title; and from there coveted the position of abbot in a monastery.

So, just like laypeople, they were engaged in the ways of the world, which resemble the waves of a lake: one passes, another follows it, a bit higher than the first, a third arrives, even higher, and in this way the waves break without end, each one higher than the one preceding it. Isn't it better to stop this process immediately by entering completely the way of Dharma? If we do not, we may wrap ourselves in a monk's robe and possibly become famous, but we will be living according to the eight principles of this world that bind us to samsara.* We will have disciples who will increase our material goods, then we must find attendants to take care of our goods, so our worries and responsibilities will increase. Unless our mind is completely disciplined, our practice of Dharma will become, at the very least, questionable. Because we have disciples, we must still teach the Dharma but we will know that we are not really living it. Or perhaps we will fool ourselves and will not live according to the Dharma but instead according to the eight principles of the world.

---

*The "eight principles" are: love of praise; rejection of blame; desiring gain; fearing loss; liking comfort and luxury; fearing discomfort and poverty; taking in all that is pleasant; rejecting all that is painful.

If even a person in this position, who is supposed to know the Dharma, can behave like this and let himself live in a way contrary to what the Dharma advocates, how then can someone who does not know the Dharma escape this fate? Our life passes, we have wasted it, and we arrive at the end frightened. We would finally like to practice Dharma, but no longer have the strength. A life wasted in this way is often summed up like this: the first twenty years pass with enthusiasm, without thinking of the Dharma; the next twenty years pass with the vague desire to practice but without having the time to do so; then the last twenty years pass in regret of our inability to practice the Dharma.

So, here we are—our life has passed in emptiness, not the search for Emptiness!

If the mind is not occupied with and completely absorbed in the Dharma, no practice has any meaning. As a master said, "If the mind is not totally immersed in the Dharma, counting mantras serves only to wear down one's fingernails."

There is no time to lose—circumstances can suddenly turn unfavorable. Whatever outward facade you have or whatever others think of you, the most important thing is to be your own witness. Be your own witness to avoid regret and remorse, and from time to time do a thorough internal examination! Having discipline is very important. If life waited for our good intentions there wouldn't be any problem, but life does not wait, time passes—"the life of the three worlds is as impermanent as autumn clouds."

There is no real possibility for us to practice all the 84,000 teachings of the Buddha; even the great saints like Nagarjuna were not able to do this. At the beginning of his spiritual evolution, Nagarjuna was an ordinary being, like us; only his continued efforts made him gradually progress and increase his possibilities, and he became what he was. Without effort, none of the great masters would have become what they were. Remembering this should encourage us, because it said in the *Bodhicharyavatara* that "even flies have the potential to become a Buddha." If a fly has this possibility, how much faster can we arrive at buddhahood! This should give us great encouragement, we must use our potential and not postpone this effort until later. All opportunity is within reach if we put ourselves to work immediately; through this we will bring about the transformation of the mind.

Our bodily actions and our speech are subject to the power of the mind. Even for a person living on the ordinary plane of mundane existence, commonplace wrong deeds can be transformed by the mind. And even if such a person's mind is in dense ignorance yet has a small degree of strong resolve, bad deeds will turn into to good ones. Furthermore, a person who is a bit more evolved with an average amount of determination can transform mediocre deeds into very good ones. Mental development is extremely important.

We must initially aim neither too high nor too far in our practice of Dharma. Begin by practicing small things with your present ability (just as a person who desires to eat very well but, without the means to do so, must eat whatever is available to survive), without throwing yourselves into higher practices. The small things will transform themselves, little by little; drop by drop, the ocean is formed. Do not look too far ahead, but begin the journey now.

What are we going to practice? There is the Hinayana Dharma and the Mahayana Dharma; the Sutrayana, the Paramitayana, and the Tantrayana. The Dharma we have in Tibet embraces the Sutrayana, the Paramitayana, and the Tantrayana. In order to practice it, we must have knowledge of it; and in order to know it we must hear it being taught. I assume that you have come here with this motivation. This teaching of Lama Thogs-med bsang-po condenses the practices of the bodhisattva into thirty-seven verses. As you listen to these verses, keep this aspiration in mind: "In this place where Gautama Buddha was shown enlightenment, I will develop in myself the spirit of bodhichitta and I will accumulate the merits to attain the state of full enlightenment and buddhahood."

This is the goal. To achieve it, you must follow this teaching with great attention.

Sixth Practice

To rely on a spiritual friend who has eliminated all illusions, whose competence in the teachings and practice is complete, and whose qualities increase like the crescent moon; to cherish this perfect guru more than one's own body is a practice of the bodhisattva.

It is not enough to remain in solitude. We must completely uproot illusions and the only way to do this is to arrive at the realization of shunyata: prajna. The realization of emptiness can only be attained by *shamatha* (calm, one-pointed concentration) and *vipashyana* (insight) together. This is the only possible method. Without this, living virtuously, reciting mantras and prayers—all of which is advantageous to us—will offer only temporary benefit. To arrive at a permanent state of well-being, at perfect peace, the root of illusion must be destroyed.

The training of the mind helps us in this manner:

Shila protects us, like good armor.
Prajna is the weapon that can defeat our enemies.
Samadhi is the strength necessary to wield the weapon.

The "enemies" mentioned above are erroneous views, the illusions that lead us from beginningless time. We cannot think only of today, we must foresee that the battle will be long—it will continue tomorrow, for our entire life, and also other lifetimes. Protected by the shield of shila, we can develop our powers of prajna and samadhi. Once this work is done we can take up the fight.

Consequently, to increase our virtuous qualities, we need a guardian to encourage our effort. We should regard the spiritual friend who guides us on the path as more precious than our own life.

Even in an ordinary school we insist on certain qualities in a teacher, such as knowledge of his subject, a good character, and his potential for setting a good example by his own behavior. We should insist even more on such qualities from the person who teaches us the way to attain eternal well-being.

According to the *Alankara Sutra* by Maitreya, a guru must possess ten principal qualities: "He must be disciplined and peaceful, possess equanimity and a supreme degree of all normal qualities, never weaken in his efforts. He should be rich in teachings, capable of exposing the clear truth of shunyata and the method of his research. His speech should always be wise. He should always be kind and should never let himself become discouraged." We must find and follow a master who possesses these qualities. We ourselves should have the nine qualities of a disciple, in summary: we should have the attitude of a wise child, not behave egotistically, follow the guru's instructions, fulfill his desires, and be devoted to him.

If the student has this spirit and the guru is qualified, the student is sure to progress. The closer the disciple feels to the master and the more he or she trusts in them, the more fruitful the relationship will be. We must be able to see the master as the Buddha, and respect and serve the guru as a Buddha. The guru should assess a student before accepting him or her as their disciple. Especially in tantrism, gurus and disciples must have a perfect understanding of their complementary qualities. It is not the title of "lama" or "tulku" that makes a good guru, but the qualities I have spoken of, and if we do not find these qualities in the guru we must leave him without hesitation, regardless of his title. If you do not find these qualities in Gyalwa Rinpoche* then you must also abandon him. We do not have to respect a master because of his rank or position, we have total freedom of choice. The Dharma embodies this total freedom. Whatever master or tradition we follow, the mind must keep its openness and freedom, this is its nature. If we force it, the mind will become obstinate and react by rebelling. It is only in freedom that the mind can discipline itself.

Everything we do must be done with thoughtfulness. If we engage ourselves only superficially in the practice of Dharma, we will become dissatisfied and critical of it. It is much easier to criticize something when we do not understand it at all. So let us choose in full freedom and with great care our Guru Vajradhara, for once we have chosen them, we must follow them in all things without egoism; we must surrender ourselves to the teachings they give us and let the guru determine what those teachings should be.

So take care not to align yourself out of enthusiasm to just anyone—don't shoot an arrow into darkness. The Buddhadharma must not be followed blindly; each point of doctrine and method has a sound basis and reason for being. Even in this degenerate age, the Buddhadharma has lost none of its

---

*The Dalai Lama.

radiance or perfection. Our goal is to accomplish the Bud-dhadharma, and the guru is a model whose conduct we can emulate and who helps us to live more virtuously and attain the fullness that is possible of a human being. We must search carefully for the one we will take as master, the "root" of the Dharma path, and once we have found them, we should fol-low them with an indefatigable faith.

Seventh Practice

How could the gods of this world possibly liberate us, being them-selves tied to the prison of samsara? Instead let us take refuge in that on which we can rely. To take refuge in the Three Jewels is a practice of the bodhisattva.

Before granting our trust to someone, we must assure our-selves that they deserve it, meaning that the person has the power to help us. Only when we are certain of this do we entrust ourselves to them. What, then, is the "object" of refuge that will not fail us? The Three Jewels—the Buddha, Dharma, and sangha—are the "perfect refuges" and to realize this is a practice of the bodhisattva.

To take refuge is an important act, for it determines those who are Buddhists and those who are not. One who accepts the Three Jewels as the ultimate refuge and who follows the teachings is a true Buddhist. One who does not have this profound bond, even if he has a complete knowledge of the scriptures and even if from the outside his practices appear well-founded, is not a disciple of the Dharma and is not a Buddhist.

The act of taking refuge therefore makes the difference between a Buddhist and a non-Buddhist, and the distinction between disciples and non-disciples of the Buddha is important at this stage. We take refuge at different levels of understanding, but he or she who wholeheartedly accepts the Three Jewels as the ultimate object of refuge has found the real solution.

Now I will explain the Three Jewels. The word "Buddha" (Tibetan: *sangye*) actually means "the fully developed one," "the awakened," "free of all error," "faultless." This last term comprises both the illusions and imperfections of beings as well as those of the external world. Internal faults and outward imperfection are, as I explained yesterday, a result of karma, which comes from an undisciplined mind conditioned by illusions.

What is an illusion? It is an emotional quality of the mind which disturbs it, destroying its peace and happiness. The Tibetan word *nyong mong* for *klesha* (emotion) signifies mental agitation, a concept, thought, or manner of thinking that deeply distresses the mind. This state, if it dominates the mind, renders it impossible to control without discipline, and brings about actions that will create karma.

The production of karma depends on the control, or lack, of our mind. Mental control is made impossible by the presence of illusions, which are caused by ignorance. The mind will then surrender to ignorance. All internal and external imperfections come from this process: an undisciplined mind resulting from illusions, which themselves arise from ignorance—the belief in an independent self-existence.

When an individual completely masters his mind, all internal as well as external imperfections and their results are eliminated. For a Buddha, this means that the base errors of desire, aversion, and that which automatically ensues from them have been uprooted. A bodhisattva must eradicate *jnanavarana*, the obstacle to a perfect understanding of the essence of existence. Even the great bodhisattvas still have a thin veil separating them from total omniscience. When the perfection of understanding is obtained, the entirely free mind opens up, spreads out. Complete enlightenment prevents the process of ignorance, explained above, from beginning again, and a person who has attained this supreme state with all of its potentialities of understanding is a fully realized Buddha.

The state of buddhahood does not come spontaneously; it demands a voluntary development of the mind. Buddhahood is not without cause, it is not a permanent and intrinsic state of being. The Dharma teaches that sentient beings do not remain in a static state. All Buddhas, like Shakyamuni who became enlightened right here in Bodh Gaya, were once like us. They were in the same state of consciousness that we are now in. Then, little by little progressing on the path, gradually stripping away all their imperfections, developing virtuous qualities one by one, they finally became Buddhas.

Abandoning faults and attaining virtue are principally accomplished by the mind, which has an extraordinary range of possibilities. While you listen to me and look at me, you are simultaneously perceiving different things, different objects of knowledge: sounds, colors, forms, etc. These come from sensory perception and turn into mental understanding, which we have always described as belonging to the brain. This mental understanding is the most important. Each sensory perception—seeing, touching, hearing—has its own function; but the results of their findings in the end take place in the mind and an idea arises: "I have seen," "I have felt," etc. The concept of "I" and "self," this preeminent factor, is therefore mental. It is the consciousness that draws conclusions.

There are different levels of mental consciousness, from coarse to very subtle. At this moment our consciousness is at a certain level of activity. During the dream state, it will be at another, more subtle level; it will attain yet another in the decline of life, and will pass through other stages until the highest and most subtle takes place at the moment of death. There we arrive at an altogether different state of consciousness. At the final instant, the unrefined consciousness will disappear, while externally the cessation of breathing seems to announce death. But, in reality, life continues in the most subtle state of consciousness. The real nature of the mind is this most subtle level of consciousness, free from all illusion, because illusions awaken and act on the less refined stages of consciousness that have disappeared.

This most subtle state of the mind is free of all imperfection, which clearly illustrates that errors are temporary. The ultimate nature of the mind does not have any pollution.

No one is angry permanently; if aversion lasted, the mind of an easily-angered person would be irritated all the time. Even if someone is susceptible to fits of extreme anger, they subside and irritation or aversion subsides. The anger was temporary; therefore, the flaws of the mind are not inherent to the mind.

Desire, attachment, and jealousy are of different "families." Such illusions, as powerful as they may appear, can be destroyed and avoided. For example, let's take aversion: the illusion of antipathy awakens in response to an object that appears unpleasant to us, making us want to push it away, turn away from it, or see harm done to it. This is a very frustrated state of mind. On the other hand, the mind produces a feeling of tenderness, well-being, and desire for closeness toward a pleasant object. These two opposite attitudes of the mind cannot simultaneously coexist.

The qualities of the mind have different natures and are often diametrically opposed in this way. Harmful states of mind are brought on by ignorance, and so are not supported by a sound understanding. The notion of inherent existence is due solely to ignorance of the true nature of ultimate reality.

The consciousness that perceives each thing as existing separately is false. Actually, nothing exists in this way. When we set out to investigate things on this basis, the more deeply we look into objects and concepts, the more they dissolve. Generally, if we examine an object intensely, it becomes more and more defined and precise. But when the object does not actually exist, what we "thought" existed vanishes. A smooth talker may impress us at first with dazzling conversation that lacks any substance, and upon coldly analyzing it we may conclude that what they are saying may be the opposite of the truth. It is the same with the existence that we attribute to each thing. When we discover this, ignorance begins to disappear and the craving that we felt for other people and things loses its power.

Due to illusion, the faults of the mind seem insurmountable at first. But because they depend on an illusionary base, they are temporary. Good and virtuous qualities of the mind are not supported by false conceptions, so that we have two states of mind, one of which excludes the other, one having a solid foundation that the other totally lacks. It follows that when we endeavor to develop the positive qualities of the mind, which have a true base, the negative ones, which lack a true foundation, disintegrate little by little until they have completely disappeared. When warmth and light increase, coldness and darkness diminish.

However, at the beginning of our practice the negative forces can sometimes gain ground. If our basic attitude is one of disrespect, we will have a difficult time cultivating devotion. Even if we are able to show generosity toward other beings and forget our egoism for a while through strenuous effort, we will weary of the pressure of this effort and fall back into our old egocentric habits. Why does this happen? Because we have not yet built this internal work on a sound foundation, the realization of the inherent and real nonexistence of "self," and because our virtuous actions come only from a obscured view tainted with samsaric illusions. This is why we must use method and wisdom at the same time. Only this will allow the positive forces to increase without fail, and once we adopt this practice it will contribute to the infinite development of virtuous states of mind and to the progressive destruction of negative forces. When the positive qualities are perfectly accomplished through this process, we will attain liberation and buddhahood.

The Buddha Shakyamuni is an example of one who has attained this state. According to the Theravadins, he was a bodhisattva during the first part of his life. He attained the state of complete illumination under the bodhi tree, thus becoming the Buddha. He remained living in his earthly body until the parinirvana, which propelled him into the *dharmadhatu*, signifying the total cessation of his ordinary consciousness.

According to the Mahayana, this is not exactly what happened. Without a physical aspect, the Buddha abides in the dharmakaya, and from there he manifests in different forms in order to continually help all sentient beings, not only those of our world but beings from other, unknown worlds. The Buddha Shakyamuni *lives,* and in this way is a manifestation of the dharmakaya. So the Mahayana says that while Gautama Buddha was born a prince and may have passed through different events, his "manifest" existence was a bit like a role he played to be an aid and an example for us. But in fact he was already enlightened.

The mind of such a Buddha is known as *jnanadharmakaya,* the most subtle of mental states, in which all obstacles to seeing the ultimate nature of all existence—shunyata, emptiness—have been completely eliminated. Absorbed in emptiness, jnanadharmakaya simultaneously perceives the ultimate nature of each phenomenon at the same moment that it appears. This state of mind is enveloped in a subtle body (which we cannot imagine in our current state of consciousness) called the sambhogakaya (body of bliss), which exists until the end of samsara. Originating from the sambhogakaya is the nirmanakaya (body of form), which manifests itself through different beings and in different worlds.

To take refuge in the Buddha is to take refuge in his three bodies. Do you now clearly understand the meaning of taking refuge in the Buddha?

Let us now speak of Dharma. The ultimate Dharma is the cessation of all imperfection, the elimination of all illusion through the realization of emptiness. The ultimate Dharma is the true path of the Buddhas and the great bodhisattvas, the *aryabodhisattvas* who have nearly arrived at buddhahood. (We use the word "path" because there are progressive degrees of realization; buddhahood is the perfection of this process.) *Aryashravakas* and *aryapratyekabuddhas* have also arrived at true cessation and their realization also represents the ultimate Dharma.

To be able to abandon all error and all obscurity (which can only be done through the realization of emptiness) is the object of "taking refuge in the Dharma." So the Dharma is the true refuge and when we attain it we are liberated from all suffering and all limitation. The Dharma is the most important refuge.

"Sangha" refers to those who test this true cessation and this true path. The *aryasangha*, or ultimate sangha, consists of those who have realized shunyata.

These then are the three objects of refuge of the disciples of the Buddhadharma.

When we regard these three objects as being outside ourselves, it is said that we are taking refuge in the cause-refuge the way a timid or frightened person seeks the support of a strong person. But our final goal should be attain this state ourselves, for it is the object of our initial desire—"to be free of suffering and to attain happiness." This must be an internal act, for all suffering comes from karma, illusion, and ignorance. Only in progressively putting an end to ignorance, illusion, and karma—which proceeds from one (karma) to the other (illusion), and fundamentally derives from the cause of illusion (ignorance)—will we be liberated from all suffering.

The notion of only an outward presence of Buddha, Dharma, and sangha is not enough. We must see the Three Jewels as a system to examine the ways we can attain our goal. We must look at the Buddha as a master or a physician and confidently follow his instructions or prescriptions, which is the Dharma, and make our practice in accordance with them.

We cannot attain the ultimate Dharma immediately. But as soon as we enter into the path we can begin to develop the qualities that will guide us and step by step we will finally attain the infallible and supreme Dharma. In order to do this we must start at the beginning—that is, by abandoning the harmful actions of body, speech, and mind.

The harmful actions of the body are killing any being, from a person down to the smallest insect (and even, says one sutra, the egg of a chicken!). However, in the latter example, for this to be a true misdeed you must be motivated by the intention to destroy.

Killing is the act that produces the gravest consequences,

for it causes immediate suffering. There is no excuse for killing, either out of anger or aversion. The Dharma makes certain exceptions as far as animals are concerned. While it is forbidden to bring about the murder of an animal because of one's attachment to eating meat, buying some meat from an animal that has already been killed is not a serious fault. The problem of eating meat is resolved differently depending on certain sutras; these variances are due to the diverse circumstances and conditions in which disciples live.

So we will not deliberately kill an animal in order to eat it. But if our health depends on it, we may eat the meat of an animal that had been killed already, while reflecting on the importance of a healthy and vigorous body to practice the Dharma so as to help all sentient beings. However, we will never do this only to indulge our tastebuds or satisfy our greediness, and a vegetarian diet is always preferable.

Stealing is an unwise act, causing suffering by depriving another person of their possessions.

Acts of sexual misconduct are ranked among the principal faults of the body. In general, this means adultery, the act of having physical relations with someone other than your own spouse. A great deal of trouble in daily life comes from this; from the most advanced societies of developed countries to the most "primitive," most arguments occur because of problems caused by these kinds of relations.

To lie relates to the habit of deceiving and misleading others. However, if the life of a sentient being or the Dharma can be protected by a lie, there is some excuse to be less than completely honest.

Malicious gossip and slander create disputes and opposition between individuals or groups of people, and can bring about serious intolerance. The masters say that when we are with others we must look after our tongue, and when we are alone, after our mind.

Trivial speech, talkativeness, idle chatter, are useless. Such talk is generally centered around desire, attachment, or aversion, and only increases our illusions.

Greed, evil intentions, and false views come from the mind. The mental attitude of greed consists of always wanting what others possess and never being content with little. Evil intentions manifest by the mental attitude of aggression toward others. False views are those that deny the law of karma, reincarnation, and the truth of the Three Jewels.

Abandoning this group of ten harmful actions is equal to acquiring ten corresponding virtues. This is the first step on the path of Dharma. With this base, the correct attitudes of body, speech, and mind can be developed. We then add the aspiration of bodhichitta and other practices that will assure our development. When we awaken to the view of impermanence and develop mindfulness of it, and when we recognize the nature of suffering, we will seek shunyata, emptiness, the ultimate truth. In this way, progressively, the ultimate Dharma will be born within us. This is why the true refuge, the Dharma, can save us.

The Dharma also means the practice of all that allows us to attain this goal.

The sangha must set an example and be a model for us. It is extremely encouraging to hear the stories of past gurus, of sentient beings developing bodhichitta and realizing shunyata. If others have been able to do it, then why can't we? This is a source of great inspiration. So the sangha provides an example that helps guide us in our practice of Dharma.

We know from various stories of the aryabodhisattvas' heroic efforts to help sentient beings. We should be inspired to follow their footsteps exactly. This should sum up our attitude regarding the sangha.

The Buddha is the master who guides us, the Dharma is the true refuge, the sangha is the helpful friend. To take refuge in the Three Jewels is a practice of the bodhisattva.

Eighth Practice

The intolerable suffering of the lower realms is said by the Buddha to be the fruit of karma; therefore, to never commit unwise deeds is a practice of the bodhisattva.

Good karma creates the marvelous deeds of the Buddhas and bodhisattvas, but negative karma leads to the various and infinite suffering of the three lower realms. All this suffering comes from a distorted mind. The countless forms of living beings that we know of, and those we do not perceive, are the effects of karma (and the inhabitants of the hell realm, whether or not those that are described in the *Abhidharma,* are the products of karma). As there is such a great variety of appearances, forms, and ways of existing among the beings that we can see, we can deduce that countless other varieties of beings also populate other worlds.

The suffering of animals is immediately apparent, for example, in goats and lambs slaughtered by the butcher, unable to save their own lives. Animals are harmless, they are totally powerless, possessing nothing but the bit of water or food we give them. They are so simple, so stupid, ignorant, and defenseless, that men really have no right to hunt and kill them for food. Cows, horses, mules, and other animals have a dismal life and a dismal fate. They cannot benefit from any of the faculties accorded us—even veterinary treatments are for our profit rather than theirs. In the case of an accident that occurs through no fault of our own, a human being has recourse to the law. An animal that has had its legs broken in such an accident has only the right to be killed; no justice exists for it. The life of an animal is only suffering.

Let us put aside the suffering of hell and that of the realm of the *pretas,* as we can never be sure that we will not be reborn there. A virtuous life is an absolute guarantee of human rebirth. The Buddha himself taught that suffering was the fruit of wrongful actions and the Buddha teaches only the truth.

In reflecting on this and trusting in the Buddha, we will abandon all wrongful actions even at the risk of our own life.

Up until now, we have traveled the Narrow Way of the path of humanity. What follows is the Middle Way of the path of humanity.

Ninth Practice

The happiness of the three worlds is like the dew on the tip of a blade of grass, disappearing in an instant. To aspire to supreme, immutable liberation is a practice of the bodhisattva.

We sometimes think we have found perfection in samsara, but this perfection is as ephemeral as a drop of dew on a leaf, shining brilliantly one moment, gone the next. Liberation is the only state of stable and permanent happiness. To not regard samsaric happiness, insubstantial and temporary, as real is a practice of the bodhisattva.

Compared to other forms of life, human life is happy. Yet we cannot be fully confident even in human life, for unless we have left the samsaric state and are free, we are always subject to falling back into the lower realms. During the first weeks of existence in the uterus, the embryo, being unconscious, does not experience this unpleasant state. But as soon as the fetus forms, the discomfort of its situation manifests. In fact, the child suffers from the time of conception, but can't possibly discern its suffering. A child suffers when it is born from its mother, and until its first steps is as weak as a worm and so suffers from dependence.

So life begins in suffering and continues until old age and death, which no one wants. Whatever end we come to, there is always suffering. The body was once strong and supple, but the day comes when it falls like the trunk of an old tree. When this happens, we lose self-control and are often given over to the care of hospital staff. Subjected to surgery, our body undergoes mutilations—surgeons try to operate on the lungs and even attempt to replace the heart. Regardless of all this, our life ends like a dream at the end of the night, and we leave our parents and friends forever.

The pinnacle of human life is attained at around age thirty; this is the time of fullest vigor and greatest activity. Even so, this time doesn't pass without difficulties. After students endure the worries of studies and exams, they then have to choose or search for a career. The concerns of marriage soon follow. A couple may want to have a child and not be able to conceive; or, on the other hand, may have far too many children. If we want an attractive wife with a pleasant personality and charming manners, first we have trouble finding her, and then we're afraid we'll lose her! We are anxious about our income; if we don't work we suffer, and if we work too much we exhaust ourselves and suffer all over again. We suffer from loneliness, and when we are with others we suffer from that.

So there are few chances for happiness in this brief life. Human birth in itself makes no sense. We are slaves to what we think we possess, and the mind in the body resembles the manager of a building. This life passes in anxiety and if we are overwhelmed by the constant dissatisfaction of its instability and commit suicide, this only takes us to a new birth without the possibility of choice. We must therefore once and for all get out of the cycle of birth and death.

The necessity of birth produced by karma ceases only with the elimination of all karma. Karma will not end by itself, only by our awakening beyond all illusion. Then the state of permanent happiness that comes from the total abandonment of ignorance will be attained. The cessation of ignorance is therefore liberation. Do not make the mistake of confusing nirvana with the end of all existence (as many Western books maintain). We will continue to exist, but all karmic illusions will have dissipated and this is the state of complete freedom and true happiness.

We must carefully examine how to attain this state and which illusion to reject first—the concept of "I." The bonds of desire, aversion, and attachment arise from this very strong feeling of a "me." We must analyze this root illusion using the methods of the Madhyamika school, which will permit us to "see" the true nature of existence and dissolve ignorance.

This is the practice of the bodhisattva concerning the "Middle Way" as indicated in the *Lamrim*.

Tenth Practice

Since beginningless time, our mothers took care of us with tenderness. What use is our own happiness when they still suffer? To generate bodhichitta in order to liberate infinite beings is a practice of the bodhisattva.

From the beginning of time, most if not all sentient beings were our parents and took care of us with tenderness. To realize that our mothers remain in the three states of samsaric suffering and yet neglect them would be a contemptible attitude. It is not a very high goal to wish to liberate only ourselves from suffering and attain enlightenment and peace only for ourselves. We should feel ashamed to seek this kind of happiness. Do not forget that we are like all other sentient beings. From the most primitive to the most intelligent, all beings search for happiness and flee from suffering and have as much right as we do to obtain this comfort. I have emphasized this so often.

It is always good to sacrifice a small thing in order to obtain a greater one; therefore it is worthwhile to sacrifice the happiness of one person—our own happiness—for the happiness of all sentient beings. We should regard the right to be happy as a debt we owe to all beings. In fact, we depend on one another; on the immediate material level, we depend on other beings for all our daily needs and we do not reflect on this enough. In a profound sense, the possibility of practicing the Mahayana Dharma depends on our relations with sentient beings. If they were not present, how could bodhichitta develop within us? From the beginning, sentient beings have clothed us, fed us, allowed us our livelihood; in this samsaric life, all well-being comes from them, directly or indirectly.

We may often doubt this. It seems to us that only certain friends or our parents surround us with kindness, and so we owe our help and love only to them. But whenever we see an animal killed or tortured, we experience a spontaneous feeling of compassion even though we have not previously had any relationship with the animal. This feeling is normal. Consequently, while we do not "know" all beings, to ignore them and be indifferent toward them is neither right nor normal.

Another doubt may arise: we can understand why our friends and acquaintances should receive our compassion and kindness, but why should we have this same attitude toward those who harm us? We must consider an adversary as possibly and perhaps definitely our best friend, in a very special way. His aggression is the greatest kindness that he can show us. It is beneficial to us because it allows us to develop bodhichitta—bodhichitta, the foundation and essence of the Mahayana; bodhichitta, which is entirely based on love and compassion. We acquire bodhichitta by completely overcoming the irritation or aversion that certain attitudes provoke in us.

Desire and aversion are root illusions. All other imperfections flow from them. At first, desire seems more harmful to us and aversion more harmful to others, but if we examine both attitudes more closely we will see that aversion causes serious harm to ourselves as well as to others. This feeling and its causes can be overcome by this antidote: patience toward all that provokes us. By cultivating patience, we leave no chance for irritation to be produced.

This is one of the most important practices. It ranges from everyday support for minor irritations all the way to helping us endure suffering inflicted on us by those whom we improperly call our enemies. Improperly—because the persons who allow us to train ourselves in patience should be considered our dearest friends. The guru, the teachings we receive from him, our friends and family—none are as valuable to us as those who disturb us. Legally, it is permissible to fight against those who harm us. But through practicing patience, strong and pure bodhichitta will develop and will encourage us to take responsibility for all sentient beings. Sometimes we will have to practice patience even with our friends; samsaric friendship is not stable and can easily be transformed into antagonism.

So those who wish to walk the path of the bodhisattva must remember the "Training of the Mind in Eight Verses," which says: "When he who I have showered with many things does harm to me, let me consider him my supreme guru!"

When we have assimilated this difficult point, instead of trying to take revenge on someone who irritates us, we will love him as our master and realize his kindness. When we are able to do this, we will never have any problems with others and will realize that we cannot abandon a single sentient being. Not taking care of others not only contradicts the Dharma but is even contrary to daily life, for the uniqueness of a human being, of human existence, is the possibility of altruism and goodness. Someone who does not believe in the law of karma but who lives his life doing good for others will reap the fruits that will help him in his future life, which we believe in. But someone who passes his life preaching, flaunting his beliefs and his study of the Dharma, yet who has an egotistical attitude and lacks compassion, will have wasted his "precious human life."

Preaching is not important; practicing charity and love is important, even for a person who is not religious.

To have a noble mind is a sign of Mahayana Dharma. When Atisha died, these were his last words: "Have a noble mind!" Upashaka Drom-teun-pa died surrounded by his entourage. He was laying on his right side with his cheek resting on the knees of one of his disciples, who was very sad and was crying. One of the disciple's tears fell on the cheek of Drom-teun-pa, who said to him: "There is nothing sad in this, practice bodhichitta and have a noble mind," and then he died. These were the last words of many great masters, such as Tsong Khapa—his disciples surrounded him at his last moment and all of a sudden he took his hat and threw it at the disciple who was to succeed him (Darma-Rinchen, who became Gyal-tsab-je), looked at him a long time, and said: "Have a noble mind," and then he passed on. Darma-Rinchen also declared: "To have a noble mind is the essence of Mahayana."

The attitude that allows us to consider the well-being of others as more important than our own is the only right attitude. Little by little, it encourages us to always sacrifice more for others. In the *Bodhicharyavatara* it is said: "As others, like myself, are no different in their desire for happiness, why put all my efforts into my own petty well-being? As others, like myself, are no different in wanting to avoid suffering, why then is it only my happiness that I search for?"

Nagarjuna said: "We dwell here to develop our minds with the view of serving others and to be of use to them." To take responsibility for others gives us the power of a radiant heart, a responsive and heroic heart. If we do not take responsibility where others are concerned, we will become like animals. Animals know how to shelter themselves, what to do to get food and defend themselves; we are only slightly different from an animal when we act as they do. So let us develop bodhichitta. The sutras and tantras emphasize the necessity of it.

But how will we be able to do this? We have extremely limited capabilities—"like a mother without hands who wants to pull her child from the river." We may now have a pure motivation, but few resources. The First Dalai Lama prayed like this: "May I never be occupied with my own well-being but may I always be occupied with the well-being of others! And to do this may I have the five qualities of the eye: the eye of flesh, the eye of the devas, the eye of wisdom, the eye of clairvoyance, and the eye of foresight! And the six correct faculties: the ear of the devas, wise speech, ability, penetration into the minds of others, remembrance of former lives, the complete cessation of lapses."

If we do not have these abilities we can do nothing. To be

capable of helping completely we must travel the whole path and arrive at the end. This is why I am teaching you. We have, you and I, a very strong karmic link; our gathering here is the result of causes which are perhaps very remote, lost in the past. (All stories of the Buddha emphasize these karmic ties through which master and disciple meet countless times before the final accomplishment.) If one day I attain buddhahood I will be able to help you more efficiently than other Buddhas, because of the relation we have had for so long. It is the same for you. The people who surround you and who have marked your life, "your" lives, you in particular will be able to help them when you arrive at the state of a Buddha. Each Buddha is responsible, more so than all other sentient beings, for those with whom he has had direct contact. If you understand this you can already begin to help, and then you will see that it is essential to take complete responsibility for all sentient beings.

It is therefore only in the state of buddhahood that all possibilities of helping sentient beings can flower. Even in the tenth stage *(bhumi),* a bodhisattva (who can in any case help a great deal) cannot do it completely. Buddhahood is *essential*—in this state, all is well. The unique condition before total fulfillment is the possibility of contact with sentient beings, who depend on this contact.

There are two attitudes of the mind: first, the desire to help sentient beings; second, to attain buddhahood in order to do this. From this two-fold aspiration arises the spirit of bodhichitta. A sentimental and temporary desire to help others, when certain circumstances push us toward it or our mood leads us there, cannot be called "bodhichitta." Bodhichitta is a strong aspiration, calm and stable, which should be constantly present in our mind. We must make an effort to begin. Our love for other beings is weak and limited, but little by little the mind accustoms itself to this two-fold attitude, bodhichitta develops, and it becomes the actual nature of the mind. This is the real bodhichitta.

To generate what has not yet been born and then develop what has been engendered is the essence of the practices of the bodhisattva.

Eleventh Practice

All suffering, without exception, comes from the desire for happiness for oneself, while perfect buddhahood is born from the desire to make others happy. This is why completely exchanging one's happiness for that of others is a practice of the bodhisattva.

We find in the *Bodhicharyavatara:* "All the suffering in the world comes from the desire for happiness for oneself. All the happiness in the world comes from the desire for happiness for others." And in the Guru Puja: "It is not necessary to explain further, look at the deeds: infantile people think only of their own comfort. Buddha works only for the good of others."

We have the precious opportunity of listening to the teachings of the Buddha that were transmitted to us by Manjushri, Nagarjuna, and Shantideva. Let us put these into practice by regarding others as more precious than ourselves, let us abandon all egotistical attitudes through understanding the reasons for them. The desire for one's own happiness is the root of all false views. To cherish oneself is the open door to every downfall, to cherish others is the auspicious ground for all qualities.

To impart more energy to this attitude, let's practice a training of the mind called "the exchange of self with others" and the exercise "Taking and Giving" (Tibetan: *thong len*).

Thong len is practiced like this: Reflect on the suffering inherent in all sentient beings, examine it in detail, remember and evaluate it, contemplate it deeply while thinking of its cause and effect. Generate very strong compassion, then visualize yourself in the center of all these beings, desiring to take on their unhappiness and their obstacles while wishing to give them your own peace and joy. Practice deep breathing as you follow these thoughts, visualizing that while breathing in we are bringing their suffering into ourselves, and when exhaling we are sending them the merit of our good deeds, all our peace, all our joy, keeping nothing for ourselves.

According to one of the prayers of the Guru Puja (Lama Chopa) we say: "Venerable Master, bless me, so that all the seeds of wrongful action of sentient beings who are like my mothers can ripen in me, and so that in knowing that through giving my merits and my joys, all sentient beings can know happiness."

Last Day of Teaching

That we have arrived at the last day of these teachings reminds us of the impermanence of all things and reminds us, once more, of how quickly our life passes and how soon we arrive at the final day. If our life has been very full, all the better; but if it was in vain, there is nothing left to do but to use the countering power, or force, of repentance. It is extremely important that repentance permeates our mind. This must not be an intermittent or passing feeling, conditioned by furtive emotions. It must be permanent, coming from a clear realization of our errors, a profound certainty of the law of karma and its fruits. We must make a firm decision to pass the time remaining in our lives, however long we have left according to our own karma, to follow the virtuous path, to avoid false views and what results from them, to act according to what the Buddha says, including his injunctions, and therefore honorably live out this precious human life. And so that it is truly precious, listen and put into practice the teaching of the "Thirty-Seven Practices of the Sons and Daughters of the Buddha."

I will briefly review the points I previously discussed. I spoke to you of the Seventh Practice, taking refuge, and I will now add some additional comments. We must observe the implicit rules of taking refuge; that is, to take refuge only in the Buddha and buddhahood and to not also take refuge in gods of other traditions or in certain spirits.

Another rule regards the respect we should have for all images of the Buddha and, in general, for all sacred objects. In this degenerate age, the commercialization of religious objects has become very common and this is wrong. To copy or to restore an ancient book with the motivation of conserving it or spreading the Dharma is very meritorious, but to do this with profit as the only motivation is bad. To publish a book that imparts information about the Dharma is valid, but to do commerce for personal interest and without the motivation of making available information about religious things or sacred writings is regrettable. We should be respectful in our gestures. Do not throw Dharma books on the ground, do not dispose of statues or sacred writings in just any manner.

One of the rules concerning the Dharma is to pay particular attention, after having taken refuge, to not voluntarily harm any sentient being or have any aggressive thoughts toward them. As I have said, respect is very important. Whatever form it takes and in any language, disrespect is a cause of ignorance in this day and age. While this is particularly difficult in these times, I ask you to be extremely attentive to respect.

Do not criticize the sangha; when we criticize one monk, we criticize them all. And while we may not be able to be as respectful as the Lama Drom-teun-pa, who was so attentive to the sangha that he gathered the pieces of red and yellow fabric that he found (because they might have been part of a monk's clothing), let us have deference for monks and nuns. The layperson who respects a monk considers the sangha to be a "field of merit" and each monk as an object of refuge, which implies, of course, that a monk is worthy of being this object. The rule concerning taking refuge in sangha also consists of not thoughtlessly aligning yourself to new friends, not placing faith in a person who, even though they show a certain spiritual authority, is not in the Dharma.

We arrive once again at the Eighth Practice, which deals with the law of karma and the unwholesome acts to avoid. Even though this is a practice of the bodhisattvas, it is one that is particularly important at the beginning of their career, and so this practice is part of the path of the Narrow Way.

Beginning with the Ninth Practice, we are on the path of the Middle Way. This path begins with the profound realization of real suffering. The *Lamrim* indicates that we must understand suffering clearly, comprehend its causes which are the errors leading to samsara, train the mind toward this view and develop it through the three practices: shila (morality), samadhi (meditation), and prajna (wisdom), sustained by an intense desire to attain liberation. This triple practice is a sure method of attaining the eight ripenings. Tsong Khapa said: "We can never be satisfied with samsaric pleasures; even if they appear perfect, they are the gateway to suffering.... Seeing this, bless me, so that I may generate an intense desire for nirvana."

One of the characteristics of suffering is that the more we grasp, the more we get, and the more we want to acquire, the less satisfied we are with what we already have. This permanent dissatisfaction comes from the fact that samsaric happiness is never secure, we cannot count on it lasting. There isn't any certainty in the stability of our social standing, in our affections, even in our own body. If we have an excellent friend who accompanies us throughout this life, we must leave him at death and we will not recognize him in a future life. The samsaric voyage is carried out alone. This solitude and the condition of being separate are among the worst samsaric sufferings.

The samsaric sufferings are numerous but they can be grouped into six principal ones, already enumerated here. One that I have not yet mentioned, which is by no means the least, is to have taken birth in samsara. For once this primary cause is accomplished, all the rest follows automatically and the cycle continues. Each time we eat the bitter fruit of past harvests. As illusions are the impure causes of samsara; the effects — that is, repeated births — produce new illusions and new karma.

Samsara is characterized as being of the nature of suffering and possessing five painful attributes:

1. Being born into suffering,
2. Birth, having been brought about by errors (propelled by ignorance), for this reason occurring in inadequate circumstances,
3. Bringing about the same errors in the future, caused by karma,
4. Therefore, without liberation in the present life,
5. And without liberation in future lives.

And all of this repeats itself until we are free from this existence. From the production of karma and its fruits, there is no question of permanent happiness. We must therefore leave this prison, the samsaric state, and the three practices indicated — shila, samadhi, prajna — are the true antidotes with the power to destroy these causes and conditions.

I have already spoken at length of the Tenth Practice; however, I will say a little more on the subject of the "practice of the bodhisattvas in common with the path of the Great Way."

In a training of the mind called "The Wheel of Arms" used in combating egoism, it is said: "An ordinary and external demon can cause harm, but it is temporary; while the internal demon causes permanent damage." The innermost demon, the one anchored most deeply within us, is the notion of a separate self, the greediness of "me." This profound ignorance carries with it all false views, of which attachment to self is the most fundamental. Its two root errors—apprehension of self and self-love—are the worst that we can have. They accompany and support one another; jealousy, covetousness, aversion, and so many other painful states flow from them. In meditation, it is these two fundamental errors that cause mental dullness, dissipation, and distraction.

Because of this, the true practice of Dharma is not easy. The real practitioner must be a soldier who ceaselessly combats his or her internal enemies, chief of which is this belief in "self," and which all the others surround and follow. Sometimes we are discouraged by the difficulties that arise, but we must believe that even if in worldly battles a victory is never definitive, in this mental effort a complete victory can be achieved. While winning a worldly battle does not end a war (instead it generally sets the stage for the next), a battle won internally will completely annihilate the vanquished demons.

The Kadampa Gurus said: "To combat illusions is our responsibility." Geshe Ben-gung gyal said: "My practice consists of keeping illusions at the door of my mind by using the weapon of opposing forces ... if they appear aggressive, I fight them ... if they remain tranquil, I am at peace." All practitioners of Dharma have this same difficult responsibility. A sound foundation of bodhichitta and the realization of shunyata allows us to win for all time. These are our indestructible weapons.

The apprehension of self and indulgence in self are supported by the Maras who help our ignorance produce illusions. But they are also ruled by ignorance; their power is temporary and without foundation, without ultimate reality. Sooner or later, the right view will triumph with the help of the Buddhas and bodhisattvas fighting for us with their power and compassion. In the *Bodhicharyavatara* it is said: "For kalpas, contemplative Buddhas have known with their omniscience that bodhichitta is the principal aid of sentient beings."

Even if our present resources are weak, in thinking as the Buddhas and bodhisattvas do and in making an effort to develop bodhichitta within ourselves and arrive at the realization of shunyata, we can be assured of victory despite the obstacles of our illusions. Illusions are by their very nature perishable, while the most subtle consciousness within a being has the potential of realizing the right view of shunyata. When this subtle consciousness arrives at this realization, the unrefined consciousness, which takes appearances as truth, dissolves. The sureness of this process is encouraging.

The first step is to vanquish our egoism by making an effort to see the qualities of others and cherish them. In the Guru Puja it is said: "He who leads others toward happiness can see this as the door through which infinite qualities arrive. Bless me so that I am capable of holding sentient beings as more precious than my own life." This mental attitude is the inner master, the savior of beings. It is toward realizing all these qualities that we must conduct ourselves. While walking, eating, traveling, even sleeping, we must develop our minds in this way. If we do this, we become supreme in the practice of Dharma and this is the highest method of purification. There is nothing greater than this.

Twelfth Practice

If, in the grip of violent desire or cruel necessity, an unfortunate person steals our possessions or incites someone else to steal them, to be full of compassion, to dedicate to this person our body, possessions, and past, present, and future merit, is a practice of the bodhisattva.

Yesterday we examined *thong len,* "the exchange of self with others," in a general sense; this practice lets us see others in a very special light. In the circumstances described above, it would be perfectly legal and even legitimate to use the means that society places within our reach against those who steal from us, for whom we feel dislike. But a person wanting to practicing bodhichitta must absolutely stay away from this. We must give such a person not only what he needs but everything he demands of us, whether it is our body, our possessions, or our life, voluntarily, so that he does not commit a worse action in causing us violence.

Here is how the guru who composed this teaching reacted in similar circumstances. While en route from Sakya Monastery, robbers stole the guru's baggage from him. After having robbed him and fearing that he would call for help, the bandits wanted to flee. He begged them to not to do anything to him, and said: "I will not call for help, but if you leave now, you will have 'stolen' my things which will be for you a fault, and so that you will not have to endure the consequences of this act, I will dedicate them to you, give them to you. So, in this way, you will have obtained them completely legitimately." The wrongdoers were so astonished at this that their minds were transformed and they became his disciples.

Thirteenth Practice

Even if we are beaten or tortured, we must not allow any aversion to arise within us. To have great compassion for those poor beings who out of ignorance mistreat us is a practice of the bodhisattva.

Fourteenth Practice

If, without reason, certain people slander us to the point where the entire world is filled with their malicious gossip, to lovingly praise their virtues is a practice of the bodhisattva.

These practices are similar to the Twelfth Practice. To take on the consequences of the wrongful deeds which are always committed out of ignorance is an effective way of practicing "the exchange of self with others."

Fifteenth Practice

If in the company of several people, one among them reveals a fault that we would have liked hidden, to not become irritated with the one who treats us in this manner but to consider him as a supreme guru is a practice of the bodhisattva.

And why should we consider him as our "supreme guru"? Because we can never recognize our own faults, we turn away from them and try to minimize them. The scriptures say that the master must present the Dharma to us as a mirror in which we will recognize our errors of body, speech, and mind. So when someone acts as a mirror for us, he gives us a true spiritual directive. The master both blames and praises us; both are good, for praise makes us happy, which we enjoy. But blame is better because it indicates to us our weaknesses, while praise arouses our pride. Along the same line of thought, suffering can be considered beneficial because it makes us remember the Dharma, whereas when we are happy we are consuming the fruits of our meritorious karma, and once we have eaten them, no more remain.

Sixteenth Practice

If someone who we have helped and protected as our own child shows only ingratitude and dislike in return, to have toward this person the tender pity a mother has for her sick child is a practice of the bodhisattva.

This practice of the bodhisattva is difficult, which is why I will illustrate it by a Tibetan anecdote from the "Praises of the Seventh Dalai Lama."

This Dalai Lama had a trusted and greatly favored subject. Little by little, this man acquired great personal power and turned against the Dalai Lama, at first attempting to dethrone him, then even to kill him. The Dalai Lama never used his own legal powers against him; he remained calm and tranquil toward him, speaking of him with affection. The chronicler ends the account with this: "Like a mother wounded by the knife of her disturbed child, you transformed the nature of this act by an abundance of love, and through your compassion you have held and nourished this degenerate being who wanted to harm you."

Seventeenth Practice

If someone who is your equal or someone who is obviously your inferior despises you or out of arrogance attempts to debase you, to respect him as your master is a practice of the bodhisattva.

This practice is very beneficial because this kind of circumstance occurs frequently in our daily lives. Suppose someone treats us with arrogance or criticizes us, claiming knowledge that he does not possess. Our first reaction will be a feeling of irritation and impatience. The training of the mind will then consist of sitting in meditation, visualizing this person in front of us, and in calm contemplation visualize ourselves bowing down at his feet. In repeating this practice, the aversion that we feel for this person will dissipate and we will come to love him. We must always remember that we should be the most humble of all. We are and should be the servants of all beings.

In the "Training of the Mind in Eight Stages," the Kadampa Guru Geshe Lang-ri-thang-pa said: "No matter where I find myself in the company of others, may I, from the bottom in my heart, consider myself the lowest among them and hold others as supreme."

Eighteenth Practice

When we are abandoned, overcome with sickness and worry, to not become discouraged but to think of taking on all the wrongful actions committed by others and suffering their consequences is a practice of the bodhisattva.

Two circumstances are particularly dangerous—when we are too happy, or when we are too unhappy. A person afflicted from all sides, who does not see the origin of a fault, who is sick, anxious, tormented in his mind, and separated from his own people, runs the risk of losing faith in the Dharma. But if at such a time we can think: "May I suffer for all sentient beings and take their faults upon myself, I dedicate my actual suffering to this," this then becomes a practice of the bodhisattva.

Nineteenth Practice

When we enjoy a good reputation and the respect of everyone, the wealth of Vaishravana, to see that the fruits of karma are without substance and to not take pride in this observation is a practice of the bodhisattva.

The other dangerous circumstance comes from too much well-being. If we are successful, have money, good health, and a happy family; if others have affection for us and admire us; and if, on top of all this, we are young and beautiful, we are convinced of the perfection of samsara and forget the Dharma. Little by little we commit small errors, then bigger ones. Assisted by arrogance, we no longer practice at all; confusion and the cycle of false views begins....

Tsong Khapa was awakened to the danger of pride and said: "When someone respects or praises me, immediately the notion of impermanence arises within me. Impermanence ... of the pleasure that I feel at this praise; why should I be vain when most certainly I am disliked by others? And why should I be irritated by the disagreeable things that I hear, when others shower me with compliments?" Praise and reprimand are only words, the smallest involuntary error can provoke a reproach, none of this should agitate us. Criticism or admiration, wealth or poverty, sickness or health—all is impermanence, this is the law of samsara.

Lama Drom-teun-pa declares: "It is very difficult to stay on the tips of our toes, to stand with pride, our head higher than others. It is more reliable to make ourselves humble and small." We must constantly be attentive to this. It is also important to frequently test our own motivation, for it is possible, unfortunately, to practice a Dharma of mere speech and form.

To cultivate humility, which is a source of happiness, was easy in Tibet, given our social structure and the admiration we have in our land for this quality. It is less easy in Western countries, because the social system does not favor it, and in daily and especially professional life to be humble "devalues" us. Nevertheless, wherever we are we must practice this virtue which is essential in the Mahayana Dharma.

Twentieth Practice

Unless the aggression of our inner adversaries ceases, the more we fight them the more they multiply. Similarly, until we have mastered our own mind, negative forces will invade us. To discipline the mind through love and compassion is a practice of the bodhisattva.

The *Bodhicharyavatara* says: "How can we find enough leather to cover the earth, whereas with a single small piece, the sole of our shoe, we can travel it in its entirety?... Wicked beings are numerous enough to fill the universe, how could we vanquish them all? But in overcoming the aversion we have for them, it is as if we master them all."

To use violence to end the hostility that causes war is not now impossible, has never been possible in the past, nor will it be possible in the future. But if each person ended his own aggressiveness, wars could no longer exist. Without this method, there need only be a single act that causes animosity in one person to result in an angry confrontation between two people. No sooner do we attempt to subdue the antagonists through violence than their numbers increase, each invoking his "just cause" to fight. In this way, the conflict spreads and becomes war.

There may be in the world and in certain regions periods of calmness, but the feeling of separation and aggression remains latent and fundamental, and conflicts reappear at the slightest opportunity. This proves that there is something wrong with the way we practice the Dharma. That which is "political" is subject to corruption, but the source of this corruption is within each human being. Therefore our personal work is to vanquish all vindictive feelings within ourselves. This can be done through the power of love and compassion.

Tsong Khapa speaks the "Praise of Buddha" in this way: "Without brandishing a sword and without carrying armor, the million-strong army of Mara is conquered by You alone. Who other than You can know this victory? It is the result of immense compassion and intense love."

If no one attempts to bring about peace, conflicts worsen. But a single calm and peaceful person can bring about much peace. Free of internal agitation, we can discuss things effectively and in this way find solutions. We must calm this inner agitation that always comes from an emotion brought about by attachment, aversion, or desire. To master one's mind is a practice of the bodhisattva.

Twenty-first Practice

The nature of sense pleasures is like that of saltwater: the more we drink, the more our thirst increases. To abandon the objects toward which desire arises is a practice of the bodhisattva.

The objects of our desire can easily be compared to saltwater; the more we indulge in them, the more our craving for them increases without ever being satisfied, so much so that all the pleasures and joys that come from desire or attachment are profoundly harmful.

The most obvious example is that of sexual pleasure. It seems to be immediate bliss, but it turns out be suffering and a cause of suffering. We can compare it to hives; when we suffer from this sickness, scratching ourselves offers relief. But this only makes us want to scratch more and this eventually causes an infection. To scratch yourself when you have hives is pleasant, but to not have hives is better.

Samsaric pleasures are pleasant but temporary; to be free of desire for them allows a state of true happiness. Nagarjuna says in the *Ratnavali:* "The more you enjoy the object of your desire, the less it gives you satisfaction. Seeing this, whatever the object of your desire is, abandon it immediately."

Until now the practices of the bodhisattva have concerned relative bodhichitta. Now we will speak about ultimate bodhichitta and we will comment on two meditations: space as meditation and illusion as meditation.

Twenty-second Practice

All that appears comes from an illusion of the mind and the mind itself is from beginningless time without inherent existence, free from the two extremes of manifestation (eternalism and nihilism) and beyond all elaboration. To understand this nature (Tathata) and to not conceive of subjects and objects as really existing is a practice of the bodhisattva.

The Vijnanavadins say that all that appears is of the nature of mind. Chandrakirti of the Madhyamika school says: "Each thing that appears does not exist according to an independent nature but as a vision of the relative mind, and therefore has no absolute existence. If objects had inherent existence, the more we examine and analyze them the more they would become clear and precise; but in fact, when examined, instead of becoming more precise they become unclear, they disappear, and in the end we cannot find them at all."

Which does not mean to say, however, that objects do not exist at all, otherwise we would not have any pleasure or any suffering because of them. So they exist, but when we search for their true nature we do not find it, even while they maintain an appearance as tangible, inherently existent. This proves that objects only exist relatively, through a projection of our mind, itself relative; and the fact that they appear to inherently exist is proof that our perception itself is illusory.

The Seventh Dalai Lama said: "The objects that pass through the mind of a sleeping person are a dream, they are solely an appearance, beneath which there are no tangible objects, they are an idea of the mind. In the same way, self and others, samsara and nirvana, are designated by the name and the knowledge we have of them. Therefore there is no inherent existence, not even that of the smallest particle."

Each phenomenon seems to truly exist on the basis of its appearance, but actually it does not exist at all as we see it; this is so for the objects of the six senses. For those dulled by ignorance all that appears seems to exist as truly being this foundation ... "They come from one's evil mind. ..."

It is true, this is the way things exist. But we are deluded by ignorance, each thing seems to us to have a real existence, even though in reality it exists only by the name that we give it according to the knowledge that we have of it.

The Seventh Dalai Lama also said: "Thus, whether 'I' or other, its existence appearing to have an independent and inherent nature is a false perception. This is the subtle object that must be refuted, and to be able to refute it is what is most precious."

All appearances, pure or impure, exist only as a vision of our mind; an object is neither permanent nor independent. Similarly, if we examine and look for the mind, we do not find it. It is included in "existence" and in analyzing it we find a collection, a flow of moments of consciousness. We say, "My consciousness," and it seems evident to us, whole and real. But in order to analyze it we must divide it into each of its "moments." The mind therefore does not exist as a whole, there is not a "totality" separate from the parts (moments of consciousness) and obviously none of the parts (moments) can be the whole. The whole ("my" consciousness, the mind) exists in relation to the parts (moments), but we find nothing solid that can be this whole.

From beginningless time the mind has been free of the two extremes: inherent existence and total nonexistence. It is truly what we can call non-self-existent, and, as the Seventh Dalai Lama said, the foundation of samsara and nirvana is a simple projection of our mind, a designation made by it. Samsara and nirvana are of the nature of the mind, which itself has never been born and cannot be destroyed.

Here is an excerpt from "Chant of a Guru": "I am a meditator on the space without birth. Nothing exists ... neither sounds nor forms ... I am a great liar who sees all appearance as the game of illusion. Marvelous is the union of appearance and emptiness. I have found the truth of interdependence which does not deceive."

This meditator says he is a great liar because all things appear to him as real, while at the same time he realizes that they are not. If each thing had a real existence, permanent and independent, there could not be any contradiction within them. A tree covered with brilliant flowers in springtime would not in autumn become a sad skeleton, bare and stripped. If the beauty of the tree really inherently existed, it would always be there, and if the tree existed it could not be at one time beautiful, then bleak. It is the same with young and beautiful people who become old and ugly. If our mind of ignorance and defilement inherently existed, it could not become the mind of a Buddha.

But everything changes—beauty into ugliness, youth into old age, fault into virtue—which proves that nothing really exists. A tangible existence would imply that there would not be any change at its base and that this base would be without cause, or effect. But there is cause and effect, good and bad, beauty and ugliness, which can only appear on a base without real existence. This being the case, the marvel occurs: a vast variety of phenomena appear, changing according to causes and circumstances. Because the nature of these numerous appearances is emptiness, they can manifest under different aspects. This indicates that emptiness does not deny appearances, and that appearances do not refute emptiness.

This is very difficult to realize, but we must accustom our minds to it. We must at times meditate on appearances and at other times on emptiness. We must always balance our spiritual practices and in this way we can hope one day to see emptiness and appearance arise in the mind, each supporting the other, the "marvel" described by the guru whose chant I related to you.

If appearances really existed they would have to be permanent, tangible, independent. But when we make an intense analysis, all of a sudden, this living existence, evident and certain, falls as if a solid support was broken. This happens very suddenly and the profundity of the mind remains. This is a new, brilliant, unshakeable certitude. We can swear by it. Let us therefore gently establish our mind on this kind of disappearance. If our concentration is not strong, we cannot maintain it for long, but we must keep our mind on this negation even if only for a brief instant. For at that moment there will be no possibility for any manifestation to arise.

"In knowing that all the signs of subject and object can no longer be grasped, realizing this nature of emptiness, non-vision becomes supreme vision."

Keeping the mind on this negation is what is called "space as meditation."

"Illusion" as an object of meditation is in fact a post-meditation. It is the correct way to approach phenomena.

Twenty-third Practice

When we encounter an attractive object or something that pleases our mind, we see it as beautiful and real, but actually it is as empty as a summer rainbow. To abandon attachment toward it is a practice of the bodhisattva.

The true nature of dharmas is shunyata, emptiness; to realize this is the correct way to approach phenomena. When we realize shunyata, we realize the only mode of existence of all things, and in this way we realize that our usual manner of grasping them is a falsehood, a mistake. When we realize the inaccuracy of our ordinary view of phenomena we also know how to use phenomena and we can no longer be deceived by them. When we have realized emptiness we do not reject appearances; we simply cease to have an ignorant view which, through its distortion, confers real existence to objects, leading to aversion or attachment. In meditation, we search for the emptiness of a phenomenon and we establish our minds on the negation we find. Then, when we once again see its appearance, we apprehend it only as an appearance, knowing what it is in reality without the emotion created by the overburdening of our mind.

In seeing an object, we can easily think it is beautiful or see it as beautiful. But, knowing its true nature, we will not allow attachment toward it to be born. By initially realizing the true nature of a phenomenon, we see it as if it was "a rainbow in the summer sky," empty of inherent existence. This makes a great difference. The object appears beautiful and is beautiful in its relative truth, but we know that it is not real and because of this we no longer feel greed for it. The desire to grasp the object falls away and the possibility of becoming attached to it, whatever it is, disappears. For all emotion, whether caused by desire or aversion, is always accompanied by ignorance.

In the "Four Hundreds" it is said: "As the sense organs are one with the body, the power of ignorance is constant within us; consequently all illusions which exist can only be conquered by victory over ignorance."

To the degree that an object provokes attachment in us, this means we do not see its true nature. We can only abandon our attachment by realizing the true nature of the object; at that moment we will spontaneously become detached from it. To do this, we must first use reasoning on the relative plane to understand the relative nature of the object, the interrelation of causes and conditions which make it appear and which already allow us to distance ourselves from it. Then, when we have realized its profound and ultimate nature, our detachment will be easier and more complete.

These meditations are difficult and this realization arduous; the most efficient way of achieving it, as I said previously, will be to practice the two meditations alternately. Begin with analysis conducted dialectically through logical reasoning; this will lead to a conceptual knowledge of the nature of dharmas. It will only be after repeated practice of such analysis, made possible by the concentration and attention of a mind made flexible by the habit of shamatha, that we will come to realize in a clear and precise way the false nature of attachment to objects. This will drop away permanently and after a long process of investigation, the ultimate realization will spontaneously occur in meditation.

Twenty-fourth Practice

Various sufferings are like that experienced from the death of an only child in a dream. To take as truth that which is only a false appearance is to uselessly exhaust the body and mind. When we meet with unfavorable circumstances, to approach them thinking they are only illusion is a practice of the bodhisattva.

Whenever we meet with unfavorable circumstances or unpleasant moments, to consider them illusory is a practice of Dharma. When aversion for someone or something manifests itself, seeing the real nature, the emptiness, of the object bringing about the animosity will help eliminate this feeling. Aversion without an object cannot live, no more than a fire can burn without wood. To approach all things in this way is a practice of the bodhisattva.

There now remains only to mention the practices of the bodhisattva after he or she has generated bodhichitta. I will comment on them only briefly.

Twenty-fifth Practice

If he who desires awakening must sacrifice his own body, his precious human life, what need is there to mention external objects to abandon? This is why practicing generosity without hoping for a reward or a "karmic fruit" is a practice of the bodhisattva.

Danaparamita means the perfect gift, total. Many stories regarding the lives of the Buddha describe the necessity of sacrificing his own life in certain circumstances. It is therefore unnecessary to speak of renouncing one's well-being or possessions, this is self-evident. Practicing *dana* with the goal of obtaining a fortunate birth in the samsaric sense or winning the respect of others is not practicing danaparamita at all. To give with only the good of other beings in mind is a practice of the bodhisattva.

Twenty-sixth Practice

If, lacking ethical discipline, we cannot realize our own intentions, to want to fulfill the vows of other beings is simply a joke. To keep rules and vows, not for a temporal and samsaric goal but in order to help all sentient beings, is a practice of the bodhisattva.

To obtain a new precious human life or the life of a deva depends on the support of right shila (ethical discipline). If we have the goal of helping others, this shila should be even more rigorously maintained, for we must very quickly clear away not only coarse desires, but also their imprints (in the flow of consciousness). So a bodhisattva must fight more ardently than a *shravaka.*

The bodhisattva fights, for he or she knows that in order to help others, he or she must be in a favorable position, that this favorable situation can only be attained through a "precious human life," and that the more strict the discipline in the previous life, the more favorable the next life will be and a more perfect instrument to practice the Dharma in order to help sentient beings. *Shilaparamita* (perfect discipline) is what must be practiced with the goal of attaining buddhahood in order to help all sentient beings.

Twenty-seventh Practice

For a Son (or Daughter) of the Buddha who desires the rewards of virtuous merit, all adverse circumstances are a precious treasure for they require the practice of kshanti (patience). To be perfectly patient, without irritation or resentment toward anyone, is a practice of the bodhisattva.

K*shanti* is one of the most difficult practices of the bodhisattva, but it is essential. Patience must be present in all unpleasant or painful circumstances, whether they are minor, average, or serious events. If someone who is our superior irritates us, we are "obligated" to be patient, and in this instance our attitude of patience will not be of great value. But to practice patience in regard to someone toward whom we have no obligation, and who could not harm us if the opportunity arose, has great importance. To be patient in whatever circumstance, knowing that it is our karma and our mind that have created that circumstance, is the true patience *(kshantiparamita)* of the bodhisattva.

Twenty-eighth Practice

Even the pratyekabuddhas and the shravakas who are concerned only with their own liberation make great efforts to obtain virya (energy). To perfectly practice energy, the source of all qualities for the benefit of all beings, is a practice of the bodhisattva.

V*irya,* persevering effort, energy, is the source and driving force for all other qualities. In the scriptures it is said that the effort that pratyekabuddhas and shravakas make in order to obtain awakening can be compared to "what we would do to extinguish a fire burning on our heads."

Twenty-ninth Practice

In understanding that vipashyana in union with shamatha completely destroys kleshas (desires, obstacles), to meditate on the dhyanas which are beyond the four realms is a practice of the bodhisattva.

Vipashyana, in Tibetan *lhag thong*, is profound insight, that which seeks then finds the emptiness of phenomena. Shamatha, in Tibetan *shi ney*, is calm, one-pointed concentration of the mind. The union of the two is the practice of *dhyana*, which is the correct method to destroy illusions. To extract the root of samsara, to arrive at buddhahood, we must practice dhyana. There are four kinds of dhyana on the samsaric level, the explication of which extends beyond the scope of these commentaries.

Thirtieth Practice

Without prajna, the five preceding virtues cannot be called "paramita" (excellent, perfect) and are incapable of leading us to buddhahood. To have the right view which perceives that the one who acts, the act, and the one for whom we act completely lack inherent existence is a practice of the bodhisattva.

We cannot separate the practice of prajna (right view) from those of the other paramitas. In order to obtain buddhahood, we must have the wisdom that sees the nonexistence of the giver, the gift, and the one to whom we give, the subject, the object, and the agent of connection between the two. Practicing the paramitas with the notion of real existence is to remain in ignorance. Who practices? What do we practice? Toward whom do we practice? These are the questions we must ask ourselves and for which we must realize the answer: no subject, no object.

Thirty-first Practice

To not analyze our actions and feelings allows desire to arise. To examine our errors and faults in order to separate ourselves from them completely is a practice of the bodhisattva.

Attention is very important. We must be constantly alert, attentive to our actions, our reactions, and our behavior in order to make necessary changes of direction. It is in the quality of our attention and motivation that our practice will be recognized as being that of the Mahayana Dharma. Let us always remember to mind our "three doors": body, speech, and mind.

Thirty-second Practice

To never criticize others or speak of the errors that those who are on the path of the Mahayana may have committed is a practice of the bodhisattva.

If we attach importance to the faults of others, we diminish our own. Clearly, if we are beyond all passionate feelings, lucid, and full of love, we can tell others that they are mistaken. But as soon as we enter into the Mahayana, the critical mind must be completely abandoned. We only know the outward aspect of beings and we are unaware of their motivations. The world contains bodhisattvas, we do not know where they may be and who they are, and if we criticize them we will be committing a serious fault. As far as ordinary people are concerned, it is equally erroneous to render judgment. As the First Dalai Lama said, "We must always keep in mind the kindness of others toward us, even if it is involuntary, and we must train our mind to this perfect view, particularly for those who practice the Dharma. We must try to conquer our own illusions rather than those we 'think' we see in others."

We must ceaselessly train our mind to this right view as soon as we enter into the practice of the Mahayana Dharma. Above all, we must avoid criticizing other branches of the Mahayana Dharma. The masters of other traditions were and are very great. If they have adhered to other schools than ours they have done so with good reasons and for the good of all sentient beings, as was prophesied by the Lord Buddha. All criticism, even minor, leads to aggression and can degenerate into conflict, and the faults that will result will be very serious, for they will be in antagonism to the Dharma.

Thirty-third Practice

In order to receive offerings and be surrounded by respect, we fight among ourselves in a spirit of competition to the detriment of our attention toward study; our meditation slackens. To abandon all attachment to the gifts of those who care for us is a practice of the bodhisattva.

This is specifically addressed to the monks. Former masters who were great in other respects commit errors in this sense when they let themselves become involved in the affairs of the world. If we must maintain contact with our family and our friends, if we cannot leave our home, we must have calm detachment from them.

Thirty-fourth Practice

Harsh speech disturbs the mind of others, and our practice feels the effects of this. To abandon all coarse and vulgar language, all harsh speech, and all idle chatter is a practice of the bodhisattva.

Each one of us should pay attention to this. All polemic, whatever its subject, is to be avoided—particularly that in the name of religion. We must avoid the temptation of useless discussions about schools, doctrines, and different sects. The passion expressed in such talk is an illusion that will bring other illusions and we will not be able stop them from invading us. The mindfulness of an awakened mind is the correct antidote to a careless verbal attitude.

Thirty-fifth Practice

As we are accustomed to acting under the rule of our passions, destroying them demands great effort. Mindfulness of these (opposing forces) is the weapon that allows us to repel them immediately. In short: whatever we do, in whatever circumstance or conditions, to always be attentive to the situation that presents itself and to the reaction that it awakens in our mind; this, with the motivation of amending our behavior for the well-being of all sentient beings, is a practice of the bodhisattva.

However, as far as possible, let us try never to embrace these opposing forces, for it is difficult to get rid of them. If a dry forest catches fire, it must be stopped immediately or else a dangerous wildfire will follow. In the same way, if we see a trickle of water starting to spread through a waste area, it must be stopped at once before flooding occurs. Like a soldier standing guard at a particularly vulnerable area, we must be attentive to the slightest error that presents itself at the entrance of one of our three doors. "May I always remain pure of the fault of taking into consideration the eight worldly principles. May I, perceiving that all dharmas are illusory, leaving attachment, be delivered of their servitude!"

Shantideva said in the *Bodhicharyavatara:* "I ask of you, with my two hands joined, that in all of your actions be awake and attentive." With two hands joined—this emphasizes the urgency of his request. In obeying him, our behavior will be such that we can thus dedicate our merit and our happiness for all sentient beings, for all our "samsaric mothers." We should be the servant, the faithful subject of all beings, nothing higher, and this will be the complete practice of the bodhisattva.

Toward the end of his life, Gedun Drup, the First Dalai Lama, feeling weak and very tired, was a bit depressed one day. One of his disciples said to him, "Do not be discouraged, remember that Gautama Buddha prophesied that after this life you will go to the Tushita Heaven." Gedun Drup replied, "I do not at all want to go to the Tushita Heaven. I would prefer, life after life, to be reborn human in this imperfect world in order to help all sentient beings." These are truly the words of a bodhisattva, and in this precious phrase the entire Mahayana ideal is summed up.

Thirty-sixth Practice

To dedicate the merit that results from our efforts to obtain buddhahood, toward illumination through the wisdom of the view of emptiness of the three realms of action and in order to overcome the suffering of infinite beings, is a practice of the bodhisattva.

So our efforts are never dedicated to a worldly objective, not even the intention of obtaining awakening for ourselves, but are made solely to attain buddhahood through the view of the inherent nonexistence of phenomena and with the goal of freeing beings from their suffering.

Thirty-seventh Practice

The thirty-seventh practice is the explication given by Lama Thogs-med bsang-po of his work and his dedication of it.

Basing myself in the teachings of the Sutra, the Tantra, and the Shastra, I have grouped these Thirty-seven Practices of the Sons of the Buddha for usage and for the benefit of those who would like to follow their path.

Because of my limited understanding and my inadequate knowledge, this composition lacks the poetry and elegance of the language that the scholars revived, but as these teachings depend strictly on the Sutra of the Supreme, I think that they reveal the practices of the bodhisattva free of errors.

However, the immense course of action of the bodhisattvas is difficult for someone of my level of ignorance to understand and realize; I ask also of the Supreme Ones to practice patience toward me and to pardon my imprecision and whatever contradictions and inconsistencies may have crept into this text.

By the merit that I have obtained through this effort, as well as through the power of the two bodhichittas, the relative and the ultimate, may all sentient beings, without remaining within the limits of samsara and nirvana, become like Avalokiteshvara.

In this manner and according to custom, Guru Thogs-med bsang-po dedicates his merit so that all beings may develop the two bodhichittas and liberate themselves from samsara; that through the power of ultimate bodhichitta, which is the mind that realizes shunyata, and through the power of relative bodhichitta, the spirit of love and of compassion, they may arrive at buddhahood, fully illuminated like Avalokiteshvara.

Part Two

The Key
of Madhyamika

Nama Prajnaparamitayi
Homage to the wisdom that goes beyond!

I respectfully bow before the Victorious One
Protector of all beings through limitless compassion,
Who, while possessing the glory and wisdom of action,
Is designated by name and thought only, like a magical
    illusion.

In order to develop minds newly turned toward the
    Dharma,
I will here briefly explain the essence
Of the nectar of his excellent speech:
The way in which emptiness and dependent co-
    origination are united.

We all want to obtain happiness and avoid suffering. To obtain happiness and free ourselves from suffering depends on the actions of our body, speech, and mind. Because the deeds of our body and speech depend upon the mind, we must therefore try to transform our mind. The way to do this is to prevent mistaken mental states from being born, and instead allow virtuous states to be generated and to develop. We must be able to determine which states are right and which are errors to be avoided.

When certain mental states are produced, our mind, once peaceful, suddenly becomes agitated and unhappy. We feel uncomfortable, our breathing quickens, and we can even become physically ill. Such a state manifests gradually, through undesirable speech, then by actions that directly or indirectly disturb the peace of others. Emotions such as these should be considered harmful. On the other hand, all states that bring temporary or permanent happiness to ourselves and others are considered "virtuous."

Various methods are used to prevent the mind from yielding to harmful states, such as certain treatments of the brain, or taking different drugs which make the mind confused and drowsy or even unconscious as if in the deepest sleep. These methods may perhaps bring temporary comfort, but in the long run, they do more harm than good.

The best way to improve the mind is to try to recognize the nature of these disturbed states by observing how harmful they are. Similarly, in order to recognize favorable mental states, we become familiar with their benefits and the soundness of their foundation. Through the force of our familiarity with them and the validity of their foundation, and because they are qualities of mind, these noble states will grow stronger while the power of negative states will decrease. Our confidence in bringing about this positive change will strengthen our mind.

Many great teachers of this world have taught such methods of training the mind, appropriately adapting them to the place and time, and the comprehension of their students. Buddhism has also taught different methods of training the mind. Of these, I will here briefly explain the view of emptiness (shunyata).

Both vehicles of Buddhism, the Small Vehicle (Hinayana) and the Great Vehicle (Mahayana), and in the latter the tantras as well as the sutras, teach the doctrine of nonself *(anatman)* or nonsubstantiality *(nairatmya)*. Buddhists are distinguished from non-Buddhists in practice by taking refuge in the Three Jewels, and in doctrine by acceptance of the four seals which attest that a doctrine is the word of the Buddha. They four seals are:

1. All composite things are impermanent.

2. The essence of samsaric existence is suffering.

3. All phenomena (dharmas) are empty and nonsubstantial.

4. Nirvana is peace.

This is what the Buddha taught. Therefore, nonsubstantiality is accepted by all Buddhists.

Concerning the meaning of nonsubstantiality: The four philosophical Buddhist schools (Vaibhashika, Sautrantika, Vijnanavadin, and Madhyamika) all accept the nonexistence of the person as a self-sufficient, substantial entity. Furthermore, for the Vijnanavadins phenomena are also nonsubstantial, and, from their point of view, there is no duality between perceiving and perceived; all phenomena are of the nature of the mind. In the Madhyamika, the nonsubstantiality of phenomena consists of the absence of all real, inherent existence. On this point, however, the schools differ.

A true understanding of what we call the "lower schools" of thought (those of a more basic level of comprehension) is of great help in reaching a profound understanding of the "higher schools," which call for more subtle reasoning and which are intended for listeners with a greater capacity for comprehension. In the Madhyamika school there are two divisions: the Sautantrika and the Prasangika. I will here discuss the Prasangika.

We can ask ourselves if these different schools of thought were taught by the Bhagavan (the Buddha), in which sutras, and whether the division between "lower" and "higher" schools is founded on scriptural authority. The particularities of these schools were essentially taught by the Buddha according to the different comprehension levels of his disciples. In some sutras he even teaches the existence of *atman*, for if he had spoken to certain disciples of nonexistence, it may have driven them toward nihilist views or would have made them lose faith in the Dharma. If the Buddha had responded to their questions of whether the atman did or did not exist, the disciples would have run the risk of falling into extreme views of eternalism or nihilism. For them, he spoke neither of existence nor of nonexistence but remained silent, as in the case of the "Fourteen Inexpressible Views." He proposed different conceptions about nonsubstantiality that we may have, such as those mentioned briefly above.

The sutras to which different schools refer are as follows: The Vaibhashika and the Sautantrika are based principally on the sutras of "The First Turning of the Wheel of the Law" such as the *Sutra of the Four Noble Truths (Chatvaryaryasatyani)*; the Vijnanavadin is based on the *Samdhinirmochana (Sutra of the Sure Explication of the Thoughts of Sutrayana)* and the other sutras of "The Third Turning of the Wheel of the Law." The Madhyamika refers principally to the *Sutra of the Perfection of Wisdom in 100,000 Verses*, and to the other sutras of "The Second Turning of the Wheel of the Law."

The Three Turnings of the Wheel of the Law were established according to the place, time, and subject, and the disciples to whom they were addressed. If we had to determine the position and depth of various schools' "views," which scripture should we consider true when each sutra states that the doctrine it teaches is "supreme"? If we had to prove that one sutra is true and another false by considering only scriptural authority, the process would be endless. Only on the basis of reasoning can we differentiate the schools as more or less advanced. The Mahayana sutras say that we must divide the teachings of the Buddha between those that require commentary (inter-pretation) and those that can be accepted literally (direct or certain).

Thinking of this, the Buddha said, "Oh monks and wise men, as we test gold by rubbing it, cutting it, and melting it, also judge my speech in this way, and if you accept it, let it not be simply out of respect."

The meaning of this phrase was clearly explained by Maitreya in the "Four Reliances" in the *Mahayanasutralamkara* (*Ornament of the Mahayana Sutras*, Chapter XVIII, 31–33):

1. We must not rely on the person of the master, but on what he teaches.

2. Concerning the teaching: We must not rely on the beauty or the sweetness of the words, but on their meaning.

3. Regarding the meaning or meanings of a teaching: We must not rely on those that must be interpreted. Interpretation is necessary in three cases: to explain an esoteric teaching; to give a teaching in a manner appropriate to the listener; and in the refutation of an exoteric teaching. We must therefore rely on the direct meaning that does not need to be interpreted.

4. Regarding the definitive meaning: We must not rely on a dualistic understanding but on nonconceptual wisdom, the realization of emptiness.

In order to realize the nonconceptual perception of pro-found emptiness, we must first familiarize ourselves with the idea, then develop an intellectual understanding of it. Then when the emptiness of the object appears clearly in meditation, emptiness becomes a nonconceptual realization. The initial consciousness of emptiness depends on correct reasoning, which is the basis for the development of wisdom. In the final analysis, this wisdom will be founded on a real perception of emptiness, a valid experience that we ourselves as well as others have had. This realization is therefore based on evidence. Such is the reasoning of the great teachers of logic, Dignaga and Dharmakirti.

We can ask ourselves: What use are logic and philosophical reasoning for the development of the mind? Isn't a noble and pure mind the only thing necessary for those who practice the Dharma, and knowledge the concern only of scholars? There are many stages in the transformation of the mind; in some stages, reasoned analysis is not necessary while cultivating faith and devotion through practicing one-pointed concentration of the mind. But concentration alone will not develop very great energy. To accumulate infinite good qualities of the mind, it is not enough to familiarize yourself with the object of your meditation. Reflection and reasoning must also be involved; they will give a firm and coherent foundation assured by the practitioner through his or her meditative experience. For the superior type of religious person, knowledge is indispensable. But if we had to choose between being learned and having a noble mind, the latter is more important, because a noble mind is in itself a real benefit.

The pursuit of study without simultaneously training the mind would create a condition that, instead of bringing peace, will bring unhappiness to ourselves and others: jealousy toward our superiors, desire to compete with our equals, pride and spite toward our inferiors, etc. All of this would be like trading a remedy for a poison. Our capacity for study and for cultivating a noble mind must be harmoniously united. It is important to have knowledge, nobility, and purity at the same time.

In order to verify nonsubstantiality or emptiness, we must first understand exactly "what" it is that is empty. Shantideva says in the Introduction to the "Deeds of the Bodhisattva" (*Bodhicharyavatara*, Chapter 140): "If we have not, before all else, apprehended the phenomenon constructed by the mind, its nonexistence cannot be established." So we cannot realize emptiness without knowing "what" is empty and "of what" it is empty.

When thinking of a tangible object that we notice is absent, we call this absence "empty," the same way we say that space is empty. But this is not the kind of emptiness we mean when we use the term "emptiness." When we speak of "emptiness," we do not mean to say that one existing entity is empty of another existing entity. Instead, to say that phenomena are "empty" means that we have taken their inherent existence as an object to refute and that it is the absence of such substantiality that constitutes emptiness.

Nor is it that the object that is being refuted previously existed and is now eliminated. It is therefore not at all the same kind of absence as when a forest that we have crossed has burned down and no longer exists; the landscape is then "empty" of the forest. The emptiness of the inherent existence of the object is that which has never really existed at all.

Nor is emptiness the empty space we see on the surface of a table lacking the usual bouquet of flowers. (In this case, the object of negation—the bouquet of flowers—is separate from the base of negation: the table.) Rather, the base, the inherent existence of which we have rejected, is not of the same nature as the object of refutation. Unless we understand what the object to reject (or to "empty") is, or what the characteristics of a substantial entity (atman) would be *if* one existed, we cannot understand emptiness. A simple nothingness, without any sense of an object being this and not that, is absolutely not the meaning of emptiness.

But if things do not exist, why take the time to try and figure out how they should be if they did exist, only to end by noting their certain nonexistence? Every day we are fooled into believing that something is true when it is not; similarly, with the problem presently occupying us, we suffer because we think that all phenomena have a real existence, when actually they do not.

The way that the mind imagines the "I" differs according to whether we feel emotions such as desire, aversion, and pride, or if our mind is at peace. Our attitude toward an object seen in a shop will be different if we simply perceive it without wanting to buy it or after we have acquired it. Once we have acquired the object, the mind becomes attached to it, grasping it as its own. In both cases the object of reference is the same, as is its way of appearing really to exist; the difference is in the way we attach to the object after we purchase it. In the same way, when we first look at a group of ten people, while each person seems to have their own singular existence, we do not necessarily become attached to their appearance as being "real." But once we have learned (whether or not it is true) that one of them is very good or very bad, sympathy or aversion arises and at this point the mind believes strongly and totally that the object is indisputably real.

The belief in inherent existence precedes and brings with it all negative mental states, whatever they may be. The apprehension of the "self" is similar to negative mental states and in fact nourishes them. This is why it is important to be sure that the object to refute is "empty" and has never, at any time, existed. Without ignorance—the apprehension of inherent existence—aversion and desire cannot be born and false perceptions will cease. These erroneous ideas arise endlessly, like the waves of the ocean, through the force of attachment which makes us seize upon things as existent when they are not.

Nagarjuna explains this in Chapter XVIII (Verses 4 and 5) of the *Prajnamula (Fundamental Text Called "Wisdom")*:

> *When for all internal and external things*
> *The concept of "I" and "mine" has perished,*
> *All greed for existence will cease,*
> *And with this cessation, births will cease.*
>
> *With the elimination of karma and emotional impurities,*
> *   we will be liberated.*
> *Karma and emotions arise from false conceptions,*
> *Which in turn arise from elaborations about inherent*
> *   existence,*
> *And these will be eliminated by the view of emptiness.*

There has never been, at any time, inherent existence; there is no thing that is independent or exists through its own power. Rather, there is interdependent production, which has no inherent existence but brings all suffering and all kindness too, as we know from experience. Therefore, all phenomena seem to exist in various appearances that interdependently originate, yet their nature remains that of being completely empty of inherent existence. This is why each known thing possesses two natures: a superficial way of appearing and a profound way of existing, called, respectively, relative or conventional truth *(samvritisatya)*, and ultimate truth *(paramarthasatya)*.

Arya Nagarjuna says in the *Prajnamula* (XXIV, 8):

> *The dharma taught by all Buddhas*
> *Is well founded in the two truths:*
> *The conventional truth of the world,*
> *And the supreme ultimate truth.*

And Chandrakirti declares in the *Madhyamikavatara* (*Introduction to the Doctrine of the Middle Way*, VI, 23):

> *All phenomena have two natures,*
> *That found through correct perception,*
> *And that found through false perception.*
> *The Buddha taught that the object of correct perception is*
> *reality,*
> *And that of false perception is conventional truth.*

I will later explain more about ultimate truth. Conventional truth is itself divided into "real" or "unreal," depending on the point of view of a "worldly" understanding (that is, all understanding other than that of emptiness).

Chandrakirti says (*Introduction to the Doctrine of the Middle Way*, VI, 24–25):

> *False perception also has two aspects,*
> *According to whether we perceive through a clear or a*
> *faulty sense.*
> *Understanding that comes from a defective sense*
> *Is said to be false in comparison with that of a healthy one.*
>
> *What ordinary people perceive*
> *With their six senses in perfect condition,*
> *They consider as true.*
> *The rest they consider false.*

To understand the two levels of truth is very important, because we refer constantly to these appearances which bring us both good and bad. We must clearly understand both natures, superficial and profound, of the phenomena to which we are in relation. For example, if we are in a situation with a deceitful and cunning neighbor and we act according to his external manner, much trouble would result. The fault would not be in our having encountered him, but in the inadequate way we act toward him. Because we do not understand his character, we underestimate him and are deceived. If we had had an exact understanding of both his inner nature and his outer behavior, we would have been able to establish relations with him that would not have caused us any loss.

If the appearance and the real nature of phenomena coincided, which is to say if they did not have a profound nature different from their superficial way of existing, we could regard their conventional appearance as true and rely on it. However, this is not how things are. Even though phenomena appear as if they are absolutely real, ultimately they are not. They are neither inherently existent, nor completely nonexistent. They dwell somewhere in the exact middle. The perfect understanding of the way phenomena exist is the view of Madhyamika (the Middle Way).

I will now explain the way in which the object of refutation does not in itself exist or is nonsubstantial. When we perceive a form with our senses or when we apprehend something with our mind, whatever our experience, what is perceived or experienced is the foundation from which the object is to be refuted.

This base of negation and the object of refutation appear as a single independent entity, a real phenomenon (existing by itself without being an attribution of thought). This is why, aside from the direct realization of emptiness, all perceptions are necessarily false. We can ask ourselves if ultimate nonexistence is therefore impossible to establish because there is no valid consciousness that can perceive various phenomena and because "a thing" may exist in an erroneous perception.

The response is that while our visual consciousness (for

example) perceives a form which appears to really exist, this perception is, in truth, false. But because this perception is also that of the form as a form, as such it is a valid perception. This visual perception of form is valid in regard to the *appearance* of the form, and even in regard to the appearance of the form as *really existing*. Therefore, all dualistic perceptions are valid consciousnesses, in regard to the appearance of the perceived object. This is because in the expression, "a consciousness perceives an object," what we call "consciousness" is the potential of knowing which, through the force of perception of the object, manifests itself in the image of the object.

Certain eye illnesses can create the appearance of hair falling in front of the eyes, interfering with our vision, and all forms that we perceive are seen with this deformation. The perception of this deformation will be valid; however, as the foundation of this deformation (hair falling in front of the eyes) does not exist at all, the perception will be false in principle and the perfect vision of the other eye will contradict it. For this reason, the first perception is regarded as false* and obviously the appearance apprehended by such a perception does not prove the existence of the object. In fact, there is no dharma that is not posited by the mind, which is not to say that all that the mind asserts has a real existence.

If an object that appears inherently real existed in accordance with its appearance, then the moment we analyze it in detail its nature should become more and more clear, little by little, as we deepen our investigation. Similarly, in daily life, if something seems true to us, the more we discuss and examine it, the clearer its meaning becomes, and if we were to look for it we would certainly find it. On the other hand, if something

---

*See Chandrakirti citation, *Introduction to the Doctrine of the Middle Way*, VI, 24–25, on page 94.

is false, it will become indistinct and unclear when we analyze it; eventually, having no solidity in itself, it will completely fade away.

Nagarjuna says in the *Ratnavali* (*Precious Garland*, 52–53):

> *A form seen in the distance*
> *Becomes clearer the closer we get to it.*
> *If a mirage were water,*
> *Why would it vanish when we draw near?*
>
> *The farther we are from the world,*
> *The more real it appears to us;*
> *The nearer we draw to it, the less visible it becomes,*
> *And, like a mirage, becomes signless.*

Here is an example: When we say that all human beings need happiness, an image of someone immediately appears in our mind. To ensure the necessary happiness, we give this person food, lodging, and medical care which will contribute to his physical well-being, and we try to instruct him and give him a good education to help bring about his mental well-being. By caring for both his body and mind, we can be certain that the happiness of this person has been secured. But when we look for the person we have cared for in this way, we find that he is neither his body nor his mind, and that he cannot be identified separate from his body and mind.

Suppose we were to meet a friend (let's call him "Tashi"*) who we have not seen in a long time. At first glance we note a change in his physical appearance and without looking any further we say, "I saw Tashi, he is much older and fatter than before."

This unanalyzed perception is not false and our statement

---

*The Tibetan word *tashi* means "good luck" or "good fortune."

is not a lie; however, if we reflect more deeply we will note that seeing the body of Tashi is described as "seeing Tashi," and that seeing his body as fatter is called "seeing that Tashi has gained weight." In reality, the real Tashi, to whom this body belongs, cannot be seen and we cannot judge him as older or fatter. In the same way, by basing our judgment on the good and bad qualities of Tashi's mind, we say, "Tashi is good or bad." But this mind is not Tashi. There is not the smallest part of Tashi in the combination of his body and mind, the continuum, or any of the individual parts. Tashi is a designation based on of the combination of his body and mind.

Nagarjuna says in the *Ratnavali:*

> *Because the person is neither earth, nor water, nor fire,*
> *Nor air, nor space, nor consciousness,*
> *Nor something completely different from all these,*
> *What then is the person?*

The body of Tashi is composed of different parts, such as the bones, blood, internal organs, etc.; in seeing only his skin, the external container of his body, we say that we have seen Tashi's body. Which is not to say that we have not seen the body at all, because in order to see a body we do not need to see it in its entirety. However, depending on the circumstances, it is necessary to see enough of the body to be able to differentiate it from another. In separating the body into legs, arms, and hands, we discover further subdivisions into many other parts: fingers, fingernails, the top of the hand, the palm. We can continue this division right down to the smallest particles of which these parts are composed—not one of these things can be "found." If the most minute atom did not have its directional sides, then atoms could never form a mass when collected together.

Let us now discuss the mind of Tashi which we have decided is either happy or not. This mind is itself without form, intangible, capable of taking the appearance of whatever object is of the nature of consciousness. Such is the mind if we do not examine it; but if we search for the mind we will not find it. We say that the mind of Tashi is happy; but if we try to divide this mind into instants we will see that it is not a collection of "before" and "after" instants, since the past moment is no longer of the nature of consciousness, and the future moment is not yet born and therefore does not exist in the present. What we call the "present" moment is not beyond the moment already past, nor not yet born, therefore, the future. If we search in this way we are not able to establish a "present" mind. So if we search for what we call the happy mind of Tashi, we will not find it. In other words, happy or unhappy minds are only names given to a collection of former and future moments. The smallest fragments of time are themselves imputed from their parts, for they can be divided into "beginning" and "end." If these moments were not composed of many different parts, they could not form a "current."

An external object, like a table, appears to our mind as having its own independent existence. But if we analyze it by dividing it into parts, or as a total possessor of its parts, we cannot find "the table." In general, the table is considered the base of its own qualities, and in judging the qualities of this base, such as form, color, materials used, etc. we can speak of its size, its quality, etc. We say, "This table is made of good wood, but I don't like its color." This signifies that there is a base—"table"—to which these characteristics apply. However, if we investigate, neither the appreciable qualities nor any of the parts constitute this base, and therefore we cannot find "the table." So if there is no base, neither can there be the qualities (or characteristics); the existence of the base is dependent on its qualities, just as the existence of the qualities are dependent on the base.

Now let us consider a rosary with 108 beads:

1. The rosary is the total possessor of its parts, 108 beads; the whole and the parts are different; but if we remove the parts, the rosary disappears.

2. The rosary taken as a whole is one, but the parts are many; the rosary cannot exist as "one" with its parts.

3. If the parts are put aside, there is no rosary that inherently exists separate from the parts; therefore, the rosary is not distinct from its parts.

4. While the rosary does not exist isolated from its parts, neither does it inherently depend on its parts, nor do the parts depend on it.

5. The rosary does not inherently possess its parts.

6. The form of the rosary is one of its qualities and therefore cannot be "the rosary."

7. Neither can the combination of beads and string be the rosary, because they form only the base of the rosary.

Investigating in this way, we will not find the rosary in any of these seven conclusions. We could examine each of the beads separately to see if they exist distinct from their parts or not, but we would not find them.

Similarly, "forests," "armies," "countries," "states," are all names given to a combination of parts, but if we search into each part, we will not find these things at all.

Good and bad, short and long, big and small, friend and enemy, father and son, etc., are designated by their dependence on each other. Earth, fire, water, air, are named in referring to what composes them. Space is also named in dependence of the directions in which there is the quality of expansion. The Buddha and sentient beings, nirvana and samsara, are all named in dependence of their composite parts and their "base of imputation."

We know that effects are produced by causes; we are now going to search for the meaning of this production. Let us reflect on the four possible ways of existing through a cause-effect relation:

1. If an effect were produced without cause, this would mean that it would be produced constantly or that it would not be produced at all.

2. If the effect was produced by its cause, there would be no need for that which has already attained its own entity to be produced again. And if something that already exists is produced again, then this reproduction would follow a regression to infinity.

3. If an effect could be produced from an entity other than itself, it could then be produced from anything (as easily from its cause than from what is not its cause), and this contradicts the fact that the effect depends upon the cause.

4. This is why an effect cannot also be produced from two things together, because it would then be subject to the two preceding errors.

Thus, if we search for the significance of the designation "production," we cannot establish it.

As Nagarjuna explains in the *Prajnamula* (I, 1):

Neither from itself, nor from another
Nor from both, nor without cause
Is there ever production
Of any existing thing.

Although we know (and this is conventionally correct) that the cause produces the effect, let us analyze this. If the produced effect existed in itself, how then could the cause give birth to it, since it already exists? The cause, therefore, would not have been needed to produce it; the cause can only give birth to something that is not yet born at the moment of its existence. But if this state of "non-production," of "non-birth," inherently existed, it would in no way be different from complete nonexistence. So how could the cause produce it? (This would be like a child being born to an infertile woman.)

In the *Shunyatasaptatikarika (Seventy Stanzas on Emptiness)*, Nagarjuna responds,

Because it already exists, the existent is not produced
Because it does not exist, the nonexistent is not
*   produced.*

To sum up, as soon as something depends on causes and conditions in order to exist, it is impossible that it could then exist independently, because independence and dependence are contradictory.

As the *Anavataptanagarajapariprccha Sutra (Questions of the King of Nagas)* explains:

What is born of causes is not [inherently] produced,
It does not have the nature of production.
All things dependent on causes are said to be empty.
He who understands this emptiness is aware.

And according to Nagarjuna in the *Prajnamula* (XXIV, 19):

Because there is no phenomenon
Which is not interdependent,
There is no phenomenon
Which is not empty.

According to Aryadeva in the *Chatuhshatakashastrakarika*
(*Treatise of Four Hundred Stanzas*, XIV, 23):

All that is produced in dependence
Cannot be independent.
And because all is nonindependent,
There is no self (inherent existence).

If dharmas were not empty of inherent existence, it would be impossible for them to change in dependence on causes. If there were something that inherently existed, its state, whether good or bad, could never change. Let us take as an example a beautiful tree laden with fruit. If the tree truly existed through its own inherent nature, its fruits would not fall, it would not lose its leaves and become bare. If things really existed as they appear to us, how could we ever be mistaken? We are well aware in everyday life that a contradiction often exists between external appearance and profound nature.

From the beginning, we have been permeated by ignorance and whatever appears to us seems incontestably real. But if this were so, the true nature of a phenomenon would exist as it appears and the more we scrutinized it, the more it would become clear and evident. Why, then, when we look for phenomena, can they not be found and seem to vanish?

Chandrakirti explains it this way in the *Madyamikavatara* (VI, 34–36):

*If inherent existence [of phenomena] were [produced] in
    dependence [on causes]*
*[The yogi, realizing emptiness], would deny this. In this way
    phenomena would be destroyed,*
*And [the realization of] emptiness would be the cause of their
    destruction.*
*As it cannot be this way, phenomena do not have inherent
    existence.*

*Therefore, when we examine phenomena we do not find
Them beyond their fragments
[And because they are not their fragments],
We must not analyze conventional, mundane truth.*

*If by reasoning in regard to ultimate reality,
Production by itself or by another is inadmissible,
And if this reasoning proves that this is also inadmissible
    conventionally,
How then could production be established?*

Chandrakirti also says:

*If each dharma had an essential existence, it would follow
that:*

1. *The realization of emptiness by the arya would cause
the destruction of all dharmas;*

2. *Conventional truth would be able to withstand logical
investigation;*

3. *Production could not be ultimately refuted.*

It is said in the *Panchavimshatisahasrikaprajnaparamita (Sutra
of the Perfection of Wisdom in 25,000 Verses):*

In this respect, Shariputra, when a Bodhisattva Mahasattva practices the Perfection of Wisdom, he does not see the Bodhisattva as real. And why? It is like this, Shariputra: Even the Bodhisattva is empty of the [inherent] nature of Bodhisattva. The very name Bodhisattva is empty of the name Bodhisattva.... And why? Such is their nature. It is like this: Form is not made empty by Emptiness. Emptiness does not exist separately from Form. Form itself is Emptiness, just as Emptiness is Form.

And in the Kashyapa Chapter of the *Aryamaharatnakutadharmaparyayashatasahasrikagrantha (Sutra of the Great Mass of Jewels):*

Emptiness does not make phenomena empty,
Because phenomena are themselves emptiness.

If phenomena were not empty of inherent existence, the numerous sutras and treatises that teach that all phenomena are inherently nonexistent, such as those we have cited, would be revealed as false.

The thought may arise in our mind that a real person and a person in a dream, a form and its reflection, an object and its image, are similar in that they cannot be found when we look for them. This does not mean that there is no difference between them, for if this were the case then what would be the use of wanting to have a "right view" if both the searcher and what is searched for were nonexistent?

Here we arrive at a difficult and subtle point which presents a danger of falling into a nihilistic view for those whose consciousness is not sufficiently prepared. To ward off this danger, the Svatantrika-Madhyamika Bhavaviveka and his disciples use logical reasoning to refute the idea that all phenomena exist from the point of view of their profound nature without their appearance being founded on faultless perception, and they affirm that phenomena exist conventionally (by the principle that says they are what they are).

If this seems too difficult to understand, there is the Vijnanavadin school of the great pandit Vasubandhu who, in refuting the existence of external phenomena, accepts that the mind has a real existence. For those who cannot accept the nonsubstantiality of phenomena, the Vaibhashika and Sautantrika schools teach the real existence of phenomena and the nonsubstantiality of the person (in that the person does not exist as a self-sufficient entity). Non-Buddhists do not even accept the nonsubstantiality of the person and affirm the existence of an independent and permanent entity.

But if we are tempted to think that phenomena do not have any kind of existence because in the final analysis phenomena cannot be found, we would be contradicting both experience and common sense. Our practical experience affirms the existence of both animate and inanimate phenomena which form our environment and which bring us good and bad, pleasure and suffering. But if we are certain that all phenomena, ourselves included, exist, why then do we not find them when we look for them?

The Buddha responds to this question in the *Panchavimshatisahasrikaprajnaparamita*:

> It is like this: Bodhisattva is only a name, Prajnaparamita is just a name, Rupa (form), Vedana (sensations), Samja (perceptions), Samskara (mental formations), Vijnana (consciousness) are only names. In the same way, form is like a magical illusion, and sensations, perceptions, mental formations, and consciousness are also illusions. Illusion is equally

a name, it does not exist in a place, it does not reside in a direction . . .

Why? Because the name is a fictive creation applied to each phenomenon and serves only to designate it. When the Bodhisattva Mahasattva practices the Perfection of Wisdom, he does not consider the names real and does not become attached to them.

Further, Shariputra, when a Bodhisattva Mahasattva practices the Perfection of Wisdom, he reflects in this way: "Bodhisattva" is only a name; "enlightenment" is only a name; "perfection of wisdom" is only a name; "form" is only a name; "sensations," "perceptions," "mental formations," "consciousness," are only names. It is like this, Shariputra: We say "I," "I," "I," but this "I" is without reference to real existence.

In many of the sutras and *shastras* it is taught that dharmas are only names and that when we search for the object designated by the name, we do not find real objective existence. This indicates that phenomena are based only on conventional designations, which is actually sufficient to give them existence.

Let us explain this in greater detail. For something to exist conventionally, it must fulfill three conditions:

1. The object must be well known through conventional perception.

2. It must not be possible for the object to be contradicted by another valid conventional perception.

3. Because a valid conventional understanding cannot refute inherent existence, the object should also not be able to be contradicted by reasoning that analyzes ultimate truth.

The inherent existence of the object, which is not affirmed solely by the force of its conventional designation, is what should be refuted, "emptied" by what we call emptiness. This real and independent entity is what we call the "self" or atman; this is the object to refute through reasoning. As we have no direct experience of its existence, the perception that affirms it as real and independent is called "ignorance," *avidya*. There are many kinds of ignorance, but this ignorance is the root of samsara; it is the exact opposite of the wisdom which realizes nonsubstantiality (emptiness).

Nagarjuna explains this in the *Shunyatasaptatikarika:*

> *The thought that phenomena produced*
> *From causes and conditions are real*
> *Was said by the Teacher to be ignorance.*
> *From this arise the twelve links.*

The mere nonexistence of "self," the object to refute (therefore the nonexistence of an independent entity as ignorance conceives it) is called nonsubstantiality (anatman), non-truth *(asatya)*, emptiness (shunyata). As this is the final and profound way of existing for all phenomena, we call it ultimate truth. And the mind that has grasped this ultimate truth realizes emptiness.

If emptiness is ultimate truth, does that mean that it inherently exists? *Emptiness is the real manner of existing of the phenomena qualified by it.* This is why if a phenomenon does not exist, neither can its emptiness exist. A phenomenon (dharma) is dependent on its empty nature *(dharmata);* the empty nature of phenomena correlates to this. When we analyze a phenomenon we cannot find it. Similarly its "empty nature" cannot be found when we investigate; it exists only through the idea we have formed of it, without analysis of the object.

We read in the Thirteenth Chapter of the *Prajnamula* (7–8):

> *If a non-empty entity exists,*
> *Then an empty entity would exist as well.*
> *If there is nothing that is emptiness,*
> *How could the empty exist?*

> *The Victorious Ones declared that emptiness*
> *Eliminates all false views.*
> *But those who have a view of emptiness (as inherently*
>   *existent)*
> *Are declared incurable.*

And in the *Lokatitastava* (*Praise of the Supramundane*, Verse 12):

> *As the nectar of emptiness has been taught*
> *In order to destroy all false conceptions*
> *He who becomes attached to this (as inherently existent)*
> *Is severely rebuked by You (the Buddha).*

Consequently, if we search for the manner of existence of a tree, for example, we will not find the tree but its real nature, shunyata. If we then examine this, it will remain unfindable, but we will find the emptiness of this emptiness, what we will call shunyata-shunyata. The tree is the relative or conventional truth and its real way of existing is the ultimate truth. Taken as a base of analysis, this ultimate truth becomes the signification of its real nature; this is why we explain that shunyata can also be seen as relative truth.

While there is not, naturally, any difference in the nature of shunyata, in analyzing it we can divide it into four, sixteen, eighteen, and twenty types according to the bases of investigation. All are included in the nonsubstantiality of the person and the nonsubstantiality of phenomena *(pudgala-dharma-nairatmya)*.

If we have a good intellectual understanding of emptiness but we experience during our investigation a nothingness, like a wiping out of everything, this annihilation is not emptiness. Similarly, if we have only a conceptual understanding of the meaning of emptiness, this is not the realization of emptiness. This is the way the *Aryaprajnaparamitasanchayagatha (Condensed Sutra of the Perfection of Wisdom)* explains it: "Even if a Bodhisattva realizes, 'These aggregates are empty,' he is still maintaining a sign, the idea of emptiness, and does not yet have faith in the state of nonproduction."

What we call emptiness is a negation that should be made certain through the mere elimination of the object to be refuted, inherent existence. There are two modes of negation. The first, called "affirmative-positive negation," implies something in place of the refuted object; the second, which leaves nothing in place of the object, is known as "nonaffirmative negation."

An emptiness is the latter type; realization of it should make evident the mere absence of the analyzed object. What appears to the mind is clear emptiness, complete nonexistence of the concrete appearance of things; ultimate nature or simple, real nonexistence is emptiness. Such a mind has realized emptiness.

Shantideva explains in the *Bodhicharyavatara* (Chapter IX, 34–35):

> *If when we say, "It does not exist," the analyzed*
> * phenomena*
> *Is no longer perceived as inherently existent,*
> *How can this non-entity without a base*
> *Remain in the mind?*

When neither phenomenality
Nor non-phenomenality reside in the mind,
Since there is no other form that appears,
All elaborations cease.

If emptiness were an affirmative-positive negation (there-fore implying the existence of another object) the perception of it would maintain an object of reference, a sign, and the pos-sibility of conceiving a real existence in relation to this sign would not be excluded. Consequently, wisdom perceiving empti-ness would not be the antidote for all conceptions and would be incapable of eliminating obstacles *(avarana)*.

Thinking of this, Shantideva says in the *Bodhicharyavatara* (Chapter IX, 110–111):

When the mind, analyzing phenomena,
Determines them to be empty of inherent existence,
If it then needed to further investigate this analysis,
The process would be without end.

If the object of the analysis
Is found to be non-existent,
There is no longer a base of investigation.
Without a base, analysis no longer operates
And this is what we call cessation (nirvana).

When we contemplate an object (or ourselves, or others) we realize there is no inherent nature and no real existence. When we become familiar with this, the object appears to us as an illusion or a dream, which appears to exist while not really existing at all.

We may ask ourselves what benefit would result from this realization. Nagarjuna responds in the *Prajnamula* (Chapter XXIV, 18):

What is produced in dependence,
We explain as emptiness.
This is nominal existence
And it is exactly this that is the middle way.

In this way we understand the meaning of dependent co-origination to be the absence of inherent existence, and that the meaning of inherent existence is dependent co-origination. Therefore, dependent co-origination and emptiness are complementary. Strong in this certainty, we will engage ourselves in the practice of what is to be abandoned and what is to be accepted in the context of mere nominal existence, through the means of a valid conventional understanding. When this happens, disruptive mental states such as desire, aversion, etc., which are generated by attachment to inherent, non-nominal existence, will gradually lose their force and will finally disappear.

Let us look at this again. When we have had a profound experience of the view of emptiness, we will be able to recognize that all that appears to our consciousness manifests itself spontaneously as really existing and we will then understand that when attention to objects is strong, the conception of an inherent existence occurs and adheres to their appearance as if they were unquestionably true. Whatever emotions and passions are born, such as attachment, greed, aggression, etc., they arise from the subject conceiving inherent existence as base and cause.

We will become profoundly certain that the subject has a false perception, is mistaken regarding its object of reference which lacks valid foundation, and that the opposite—the realization of nonsubstantiality—is the result of a correct perception.

The glorious Dharmakirti states in the *Pramanavarttika* (*Critical Commentary on the Valid Means of Understanding*, Chapter I, 49 and 220):

> *The mind that realizes and that which falsely*
>   *superimposes,*
> *By their nature destroy one another.*

> *That which is deformed and that which is healthy*
> *Are by nature in mutual opposition;*
> *And those who familiarize themselves with a clear*
>   *consciousness of that which is healthy*
> *Completely rid themselves of passions.*

In this way, as these two states of mind have an incompatible apprehension of things, one will destroy the other. Therefore, the stronger one state becomes, the more the other will weaken.

As Nagarjuna says in the *Dharmadhatustotra* (*Praise of Dharmadhatu*, Verses 20–21):

> *Like a metal ornament stained with impurity*
> *Which must be purified by fire,*
> *When it is placed in the fire*
> *The impurities are burned, but it is not.*

> *It is the same concerning the mind, whose nature is clear*
>   *light*
> *But which is stained by the impurities of desire;*
> *The impurities are burned by the fire of wisdom,*
> *But its nature, clear light, remains ...*

The *Sublime Science of the Victorious Maitreya* (*Uttaratantra*) says:

Because the [activities] of the body of a perfect Buddha
radiate [onto all beings]
Because reality is not differentiated [as it is the ultimate
nature of sentient beings as well as the Buddha]
And because they have the potentiality of buddhahood,
All sentient beings always have the nature of Buddha.

Not only the ultimate nature of the mind but also its conventional nature is untainted by impurities; clear knowing is not touched by pollutants. This is why the mind can be better or worse and is capable of being transformed. While we easily familiarize ourselves with bad mental states (which result from the subject conceiving inherent existence), these cannot be limitlessly developed. Conversely, noble states of mind can be infinitely extended. For this reason, we can ascertain that the impurities that "envelop" the mind (but which are not the mind itself) can be eliminated, and that when they have been irreversibly eliminated, the nature of the mind will be liberation. This allows us to affirm that liberation can be attained. Not only emotional illusions, but their imprints (the last obstructions to perfect understanding) can similarly be totally destroyed; the nature of the mind will then be that of the dharmakaya (body of truth), also called "nirvana without resistance." And it can be established that liberation and omniscience exist.

In the *Prajnamula* (Chapter I), Nagarjuna states:

I bow down before the best of teachers,
The perfect Buddha, who taught
That all that is produced in dependence [of causes and
conditions]
Has neither death nor birth, annihilation nor permanence,
No going nor coming, sameness nor difference,
Is free of conceptions and is at peace.

In this way, then, the Blessed One taught repeatedly and insistently that dependent co-origination shows that because phenomena are produced in dependence, they are of the nature of emptiness and free from the eight extremes previously mentioned. Having faith in the Bhagavan, who shows us without fault the ultimate good and the means by which to achieve it, we will be equally persuaded that his teaching showing us the path of temporal liberty, beyond wretched rebirths, is faultless.

The glorious Dharmakirti, in his *Pramanavarttika* (I, 127) declares:

> *Because [the word of the Buddha] is exact concerning the*
> *principal meaning (shunyata),*
> *We will consider it [as correct] regarding other meanings*
> *(those that are hidden).*

And in the *Chatuhshataka* (*Treatise in Four Hundred Stanzas*), XII, 5, Aryadeva says:

> *If doubt arises*
> *Regarding hidden [non-obvious] teachings of the Buddha,*
> *Base yourselves on his teaching of emptiness*
> *And place your faith in that.*

In short, by knowing the teachings of the Buddha as well as the commentaries on them, whose goal is the realization of temporary and permanent happiness, we will believe in them, and from the bottom of our hearts will be born great respect and profound faith toward the Blessed Buddha and the great masters of India, his disciples. We will be able to have unfailing devotion for the teacher who shows us the path without error, and for the sangha, our spiritual friends who resolutely follow the path upon which the Buddha himself once walked.

As Chandrakirti says in the *Trisharanasaptati (Seventy Stanzas on the Three Refuges)*:

> *The Buddha, the Dharma, and the excellent community*
> *(the sangha)*
> *Are the refuges of those who aspire to liberation.*

We will be readily convinced, moreover, that the Three Jewels are the only refuges. Those who realize the suffering of the samsaric state will take refuge in the Three Jewels with an indestructible and unwavering aspiration toward liberation. Having understood, by experience, the condition of suffering of all beings, we will develop an ardent desire to lead them to the state of liberation and omniscience (buddhahood). In order to realize this, we must ourselves attain enlightenment. This way we will develop a firm and powerful aspiration (bodhichitta) to achieve this for the sole benefit of sentient beings .

If we are motivated by the desire for personal liberation, we will adopt as our foundation the ethics of the monks or laypeople and we will then be on the path of accumulation (the Hinayana).

In familiarizing ourselves more and more with the subtle and profound view of emptiness through study and reflection, this "view" will gradually transform itself into wisdom produced by meditation in which calm concentration (shamatha) and superior view (vipashyana) are united, conceptually perceiving the meaning of emptiness. The path of preparation *(prayogamarga)* is thus attained. A direct perception of shunyata therefore introduces the path of seeing *(darshanamarga)*, which is the true path, the jewel of the Dharma. This path is the true remedy; we begin to attain the truth of cessation in abandoning the coarser levels of the truth of the cause of suffering (the conception of real existence) and the truth of suffering (wretched rebirths, etc.).

Through the path of development *(bhavanamarga)*, we familiarize ourselves with the truth already perceived and we attain true cessation. Little by little, beginning with the most obvious, emotional impurities are eliminated. Finally, even the most subtle impurities and their potentialities are erased. The voyage is completed, liberation realized, and the state where there is nothing more to practice or learn, the level of a Hinayana arhat, is attained.

When our goal is to obtain buddhahood for the good of all sentient beings, the ethic that we will adopt is as follows: we will generate wisdom through study and reflection, meditation focused on the meaning of emptiness, with the motivation of bodhichitta, and accompanied by the "skillful means" of the perfections (paramitas). The view of emptiness becomes more and more profound and when it is directly perceived, and having traveled the path of accumulation, we attain the perfect wisdom of a bodhisattva, the "wisdom of the first stage" of the Mahayana, or the first "kalpa of wisdom and merits." As previously explained, we are beginning to realize true cessation. The bodhisattva must pass through the "first seven stages" or "impure realms" and accumulate the "collection" of wisdom and merits of the second kalpa. In the "last three pure stages," we gradually eliminate obstructions to omniscient understanding, the imprints left by our concept of a real existence and the subtle bad habits produced by them.

When the "third infinite kalpa of accumulations" is achieved in this way, we attain ultimate cessation, dharmakaya without fault. The three bodies—dharmakaya, sambhogakaya, and nirmanakaya—are simultaneously manifested and we realize the state of the Buddha: buddhahood, fully accomplished in the perfection of wisdom, compassion, and power.

Furthermore, the "fortunate being" who has disciplined his mind in developing the aspiration toward liberation, bodhichitta, and the right view of shunyata, and who has completed causal accumulation of merit and wisdom, is ready to enter the tantric path. If we advance on the three lower tantras of the paths of the secret mantra, we will be more quickly enlightened than through the vehicle of perfection alone. This rapidity is due to the marvelous ways of realizing the body of form *(rupakaya)* through practicing the yoga of the union of calm concentration and superior insight.

When we practice the highest tantra, *anuttara-yoga-tantra*, we learn to differentiate the "winds" and consciousnesses into coarse, subtle, and very subtle, and the most subtle consciousness which develops as the very essence of the path. In cultivating this practice, the perception of emptiness becomes extremely powerful. Therefore, the tantric path has the capability of eliminating all obstructions very rapidly.

Here is a brief explication of the method allowing us to acquire a correct comprehension of shunyata. The purpose of this meditation is to remove the obstacles to the view of emptiness; in order to achieve this, it must be accompanied by a vast accumulation of merit. Regarding this "field of accumulation," we will practice according to our personal inclination, either directing our mind toward contemplation of the general nature of the Three Jewels, or visualizing a particular object of refuge before us. An excellent way to do this is the practice of the "Puja of Seven Branches."

It has been said that at the beginning of our research, meditating on the nonsubstantiality of the person is easier (because the subject is continually present). First, we must clearly see the manner in which the meditator appears to the mind when we think: "Now 'I' meditate on emptiness." We must be very attentive to the way this "I" appears at the moment when we feel an emotion of joy or sadness, and at the manifestation of our attachment to this emotional state. It is only after assuring ourselves of these bases that we can examine the "I" in the way previously indicated.

When our understanding of the view of shunyata becomes more profound, we have an experience of it and we then realize that the "I" that appears real and independent to us has in fact no existence whatsoever. Firmly concentrating our mind on this clear emptiness, which is merely the absence of any object to refute, we practice stabilizing meditation without analysis. When our concentration weakens and emptiness becomes a simple nothingness, we must practice analytic meditation to "track down" the "I" as previously indicated. This practice of alternating analytical meditation and stabilizing meditation is a way of transforming the mind.

Having acquired by this method a comprehension (even briefly) of the emptiness of "I," we will turn our attention to the aggregates in dependence on which the "I" is imputed. It is very important to analyze well the aggregates (such as form, sensation, perception, etc.), and in particular the aggregate of consciousness. Realizing the relative nature of consciousness is very difficult but very important. Once we have recognized the relative nature of the mind, the simple and clear knower, we can gradually arrive at an understanding of its ultimate nature. This constitutes considerable progress.

To begin, meditation should last one half-hour. On leaving the session, we will once again manifestly experience various good or bad phenomena, bringing us happiness or suffering. We must also develop, as much as we can, the certainty that these phenomena do not objectively exist and, like illusions, are only appearances of interdependent origination.

This meditation should be done in four sittings: at dawn, in the morning, in the evening, and at night; or in six sittings (three sittings during the day and three at night); or even in eight sittings (four in the day, four at night). But if this is not possible, we can practice two sittings, one in the morning and one in the evening.*

Training in this way, our comprehension and our experience will be affirmed and in all our actions—walking, working, eating—the view of emptiness will arise within us without any effort. But without having first obtained the calm concentration of the mind (shamatha) directed toward shunyata, it is not possible to produce the superior view (vipashyana). We must therefore first work to obtain this calm concentration of the mind, the method of which can be learned elsewhere.

If we are not content with only an intellectual understanding of emptiness but wish to experience it fully, we must take as a foundation what has been explicated here, and then study the sutras and reflect on the commentaries which teach the profound view of emptiness, as well as the excellent explanations given by Tibetan scholars on this subject.

We must examine the fruits of our own experience with study, and hear the teaching of a wise and experienced teacher.

> By the accumulation of merit resulting from this effort,
> May all sentient beings who desire happiness
> Obtain the eye that sees reality, free from extreme views,
> And attain the peace of great liberation.

---

*The number of sessions of meditation discussed here corresponds to the daily number of sittings that a student making on a retreat on this practice should do.

This was written as simply as possible with the goal of being easily understood and translated into other languages for the benefit of those from East or West who seek the Buddha-dharma, and particularly for those who wish to know the profound and subtle meaning of emptiness but do not have the opportunity to study the great Madhyamika treatises or who cannot read the teachings in the Tibetan language.

May this, written by the Sakya monk Tenzin Gyatso, the Fourteenth Dalai Lama, contribute to the harmonious growth of goodness and purity!

Glossary

Abhidharma: The earliest compilation of Buddhist philosophy and psychology; one of the three parts of the *Tripitaka*, the early Buddhist canon which also includes the *Sutra* and the *Vinaya*. See also **Tripitaka.**

Aggregate (Sanskrit: *skandha*): The five psychophysical constituents of what is generally called the "personality": form, sensations, perceptions, mental formations, and consciousness.

Anatman: "non-self." The nonsubstantiality of an entity, whether a person or an object.

Arhat: "worthy one." One who has attained the highest level of the Hinayana; the arhat enters nirvana at the end of his or her present life.

Arya: "noble," "superior." One who has realized the ultimate truth, shunyata.

Atman: "self." A substantial entity, either a person or an object.

Avalokiteshvara: One of the most important Mahayana bodhisattvas, the incarnation of the compassion of all Buddhas. Also called Lokeshvara. In Tibetan: Chenrezig.

Bardo: The intermediate state between death and rebirth.

Base of Imputation: The elements of a phenomenon that give rise to a particular designation; e.g. the parts of a table—four supports and a top—give rise to the name "table."

Base of Refutation or of Negation: The phenomenon which is the object of the reasoning through which its inherent existence is refuted.

Bhumi: "land." Each of ten levels of wisdom through which a bodhisattva must pass in order to attain buddhahood.

Bodhichitta: "awakened mind." The bodhisattva's aspiration for enlightenment with the single goal of liberating all living beings from samsara is called "relative bodhichitta"; "ultimate bodhichitta" is direct insight into the nature of reality.

Bodhisattva: "enlightenment being." One who seeks buddhahood but who renounces entering nirvana until all living beings are liberated. The actions and thoughts of a bodhisattva are motivated solely by bodhichitta.

Buddha: "awakened one." One who has eliminated the last obstacles to enlightenment, is perfectly accomplished in the qualities of wisdom, compassion, and power, and who has attained liberation from samsara. The teachings of Shakyamuni Buddha (born the Indian prince Siddhartha Gautama, 566 or 563 to 486 or 483 B.C.E.) are the foundation of Hinayana and Mahayana Buddhism.

Dependent co-origination (also interdependent production; dependent co-arising): The term used to signify that phenomena do not have inherent existence but exist only in relation to causes and conditions.

Deva: God or deity, a being situated in one of the higher realms of existence, but who is still subject to the cycle of rebirth. Also indicates a form used in meditative visualization in Vajrayana practice.

Dharma: The term "dharma" signifies every thing that exists, each phenomenon. "Dharma" refers to religious teachings, the methods by which sentient beings may be freed from samsaric suffering. Buddhists use the word Dharma for all religious teachings, including Christian, Hindu, etc. Buddhist teachings are called the Buddhadharma.

Dharmadhatu: "realm of dharma." In the Mahayana view, the-unconditioned and immutable realm from which all phenomena arise, dwell, and pass away.

Dharmakaya: see **Kaya.**

Dharmata: The ultimate nature (shunyata) of dharmas, all phenomena.

Dhyana: Meditation, absorption. An absorbed state of mind founded on concentration (samadhi). See also **Samadhi.**

Geshe: In Tibetan Buddhism, a title for one who has attained of a high degree of knowledge and proficiency in the textual and scholarly aspects of the Buddhadharma; term for a doctor of philosophy in the Gelug-pa tradition.

Hinayana: "Small Vehicle." Also known as Theravada. The Buddhist teachings of a method of personal liberation that permits one to leave the cycle of suffering (samsara) and attain the peace of nirvana. The path of the Hinayana includes the shravaka, who under the tutelage of a master meditates on the nonsubstantiality of the self; the pratyekabuddha, who realizes the truth directly without relying on a teaching; and the arhat (see above).

Ignorance: (Sanskrit: avidya): In this context, the fundamental cause or root of samsaric existence: the mental obscurity that prevents perception of the true nature of phenomena, shunyata.

Inherent existence: The notion that phenomena exist by their own power, independent of causes and conditions. Also called: intrinsic existence, self-existence, substantiality.

Kalpa: In Buddhism, a term for an extremely long period of time.

Karma: "act, deed." In Buddhist teachings, karma is the law of cause and effect: an act, whether of body, speech, or mind, and its effects, either positive or negative, leaving an imprint in one's consciousness, which automatically brings about more actions. The law of karma compels the consciousness that is affected by it to be reborn into samsara lifetime after lifetime.

Kaya: "body." In the Mahayana, there are three aspects of the body of a buddha: the dharmakaya, " body of dharma," the ultimate and essential nature of the Buddha, which is one with transcendental reality, the essence of the universe; the sambhogakaya, "body of bliss," a body of subtle form in which a buddha resides in a "buddha-paradise," which can be perceived by a bodhisattva attaining the state of arya, but not by ordinary beings; and the nirmanakaya, "body of transformation," the earthly manifestation of a buddha, taken in order to free beings from samsara.

Klesha: "defilement," "passion." The properties or emotions that bring about mental dullness or confusion and which are the basis of unwholesome acts (karma) which binds one to the cycle of samsara.

Lama: In Tibetan Buddhism, a spiritual teacher or guru.

Liberation (Sanskrit: *moksha*): Final release from the cycle of suffering, samsara. See also **Nirvana.**

Mahasattva: "great being." An honorific name for a bodhisattva.

Mahayana: "Great Vehicle." The teachings of the Buddha that emphasize the path of the bodhisattva, which is the method of attaining buddhahood with the motivation of bodhichitta, solely in order to help liberate all sentient beings from samsara. The Mahayana incorporates two paths: the Paramitayana and the Vajrayana, or Tantrayana.

Mantra: A sacred syllable or series of syllables which manifests certain cosmic forces and aspects. Recitation of mantras is a form of meditative practice in many schools of Buddhism.

Mara: This term refers to the forces of ignorance that hinder progress on the path of enlightenment. Mara is also the personification of these forces.

Nadi: Energy channel specific to the tantric system.

Nagarjuna:(c. 2nd-3rd centuries C.E.) One of the most important Buddhist philosophers, founder of the Madhyamika school. He systematized and deepened the teaching presented in the *Prajnaparamitasutra*, using a dialectic based on reductive logical reasoning. His method of rejecting all opposites is the basis of the Middle Way of the Madhyamika.

Nirmanakaya: see **Kaya.**

Nirvana: Complete cessation of suffering and its causes, karma and klesha, and the peace that results from cessation. Nirvana is attained by an enlightened being, a buddha, who will not be reborn into samsara at the end of his or her present lifetime. See also **Parinirvana.**

Paramita: "perfection." The virtues perfected by a bodhisattva in the course of his or her development. According to different teachings, there are six or ten paramitas; the basic six are: danaparamita (generosity); shilaparamita (discipline); kshanti-paramita (patience); viryaparamita (energy); dhyanaparamita (meditation); and prajnaparamita (wisdom).

Paramitayana: One of the two Mahayana paths, consisting of the practice of the excellent virtues (paramitas).

Parinirvana: The state attained by an enlightened being at the end of their present life, in which form completely dissolves into the dharmakaya. See also **Nirvana**.

Path (Sanskrit: *marga*): In this context, designates the five stages of the way to liberation: the paths of accumulation, of effort, of seeing, of development, and of accomplishment.

Prajna: "wisdom." Immediate, experiential, intuitive wisdom that is beyond conceptual understanding. Ultimate prajna is the realization of shunyata, often equated with the attainment of enlightenment. One of the paramitas practiced on the path of the bodhisattva.

Pratyekabuddha: See **Hinayana**.

Pretas: Hungry ghosts who populate one of the three lower realms of existence. Having immense bellies but mouths and throats that are only as big as the eye of a needle, they suffer from insatiable hunger, as well as other torments. Greed, envy, and jealousy can lead to rebirth in the realm of the pretas.

Puja: Worship, ceremony, religious service.

Samadhi: "establish, make firm." Collecting the mind on a single object through the calming of all mental activity. A nondualistic state of consciousness in which "subject" and "object" are no longer differentiated as separate.

Sambhogakaya: see **Kaya.**

Samsara: The continuous cycle of rebirths according to one's karma; its nature is essentially suffering.

Shamatha: "dwelling in tranquility." Calm concentration; a meditative state in which the mind stays fixed on an object of meditation, effortlessly and without distraction.

Shantideva (c. 7th–8th centuries C.E.): According to legend, Shantideva was a king's son from South India who became a monk at Nalanda, a renowned monastic university in North India. He is representative of the Madhyamika school and authored the *Bodhicharyavatara,* an important teaching text used in Tibetan Buddhism.

Shastra: Treatises on Buddhist doctrine and commentaries on specific philosophical points in the sutras, composed by Mahayana thinkers.

Shila: "precepts." A set of ethical guidelines followed by Buddhist practitioners as a necessary foundation in order to progress on the path. One of the paramitas practiced by the bodhisattva.

Shravaka: see **Hinayana.**

Shunyata: "emptiness." The ultimate nature of all phenomena, which is their complete lack of inherent existence. The realization of shunyata results from a logical refutation of the possibility that phenomena have separate self-existence that is independent of causes and conditions and the mental designations by which they are named and known.

Stupa: Originally a Buddhist memorial monument or reliquary, stupas also serve to demarcate important Buddhist sites.

Sutra: Teachings of the Buddha. The Hinayana sutras are collected as one part of the *Tripitaka*.

Tantra: In Tibetan Buddhism, a term for various kinds of texts; mainly refers to the practice of the meditative systems of the Vajrayana.

Tantrayana: One of the two Mahayana paths; see **Vajrayana**.

Theravada: "The Teaching of the Elders." Another term for the Hinayana.

Tripitaka: "three baskets." The early Buddhist canon, consisting of the *Abhidharma*, the *Sutra*, and the *Vinaya*.

Tsong Khapa (1357–1419): A great scholar and reformer of Tibetan Buddhism, he compiled and presented the Buddha-dharma in the *Lamrim* (Tibetan: "Stages [*rim*] of the Path" [*lam*].) Founder of the Gelug-pa order, of which the Dalai Lamas are members.

Tulku: Tibetan word for nirmanakaya; this term also designates lamas whose advanced spiritual evolution allows them to no longer be subject to rebirth determined by their karma, and who may, with the goal of helping sentient beings, take rebirth in a body of their choosing.

Turning the Wheel of the Law: To teach the Dharma. The teachings of the Buddha are traditionally grouped under the three "Turnings of the Wheel of the Law": 1. The Buddha's first teaching in Sarnath, after attaining complete enlightenment; 2. The origination of the Mahayana; 3. The arising of the Vajrayana.

Vajrayana: "Diamond Vehicle." Also called Tantrayana. The second of the two Mahayana paths, it is a combination of meditative and subtle psychophysical techniques, bringing together method and wisdom. The simultaneous practice of both the Tantrayana and the Paramitayana allows one to attain the state of buddhahood faster than would be possible through the practice of the Paramitayana alone. This path can only be beneficially followed by a practitioner already familiar with the essential Mahayana principles: a firm foundation of discipline, compassion for all sentient beings, and the wish to seek the realization of shunyata.

Victorious One or **Conqueror:** An epithet for the Buddha.

Vinaya: Collection of teachings of the Buddha regarding the rules of discipline and ethics for monks and laypeople. One of the three parts of the *Tripitaka*.

Vipashyana: "insight," "clear seeing." In the Mahayana, a form of analytical meditation on the nature of things that leads to insight into the true nature of phenomena: shunyata.